H U M O R

Did You Know You're Funny?

You're In This Book.

IS A FUNNY THING

By Gordon Bushell

Published by TriMark Press, Deerfield Beach, Florida.

Library of Congress Cataloging-in-Publication Data

Bushell, Gordon
    Humor Is A Funny Thing by Gordon Bushell
       1. Humor
       p. cm.

    ISBN: 978-0-9816092-6-3
    F10
10 9 8 7 6 5 4 3 2 1
Printed and bound in the United States of America.

publishing the written word
trimarkpress

A publication of TriMark Press
368 South Military Trail
Deerfield Beach, FL 33442
800.889.0693

"This is dedicated to the one I love."
The Mamas & The Papas - 1961

*To my love, my wife, who has patiently critiqued my words
and laughed at all the right places. Your voice has helped
shape these writings. And thanks dear, for letting
me write about you as only I have seen you.*

I wish to thank....

Chuck Gilo for the illustrations,
Frank Papandrea for the cover design
and finally, John Johnson, for everything!

THEY SAY LAUGHTER IS THE BEST MEDICINE.

(OPEN WIDE)

What's so funny? Life's funny. Life's a laugh. You're living in a situation comedy but you only see the situation.....not the comedy! To prove it, here are many of your hum-drum moments turned into a book of comedy sketches. You'll recognize them. You've lived them and will continue to live them.

I'm talking funny moments like leaving a telephone message..... watching cable news......or how about that rib-tickling, uproarious moment.....sitting in your living room! Here is your ho-hum, Monday-through-Sunday existence as it might be "performed" by a stand-up comedian. In this case, a sit-down comedian.

That would be me, Gordon Bushell. I was in advertising. A writer! Idea man! Award winner! (More on that later.) If you watch prime time TV, you've seen me in action. Who knows, I may have sold you your car, your toothpaste, your cookies, your camera, your shave cream..... maybe even something for your hemorrhoids.

I started as a copywriter at Macy's. I retired as Chairman of a major N.Y. agency. But I was still young so I only retired from my neck down. My head has kept workin' and perkin' writing a weekly newspaper column. A humorous column. I've collected a bunch of them in this book so you don't have to get news print all over your hands.

So read about yourself. The laugh's on you.

Just one caution:

DO NOT READ ON A FULL BLADDER

THE LAUGHABLE CHAPTERS OF OUR LIVES

And Now The Finale, Maestro...

Hard Cell

TELL IT TO MY MACHINE

If I call you and you can' get to your phone, what will I get? Your voice greeting me and telling me you're not available? Or will I get that cold computer lady informing me, *"The person you are calling is not available"*.....etc, etc. If you have a computer answer for you, you're either very shy, or you suffer from stage fright, or you hate the sound of your own voice, or you can't figure out how to tape a message.

I prefer the personal message. It's so much warmer. But most people are very straight with their message. No charm. No wit. No fun.

"Hello. We're not home. Leave a message."

They certainly don't sound happy to hear from me. When I'm not home, I like to make the caller's effort worth their time and money. I leave messages like this:

"Hi, this is you know who. But who are you? When we know who are you, you'll hear from you know who."

"Hi, please leave a message. And by all means, speak frankly. We keep no secrets from our beep."

"Hi, you know the routine. Don't make a peep—til you hear the beep."

Recently, friends of mine named, Finger, asked me to write a phone message to replace their dull, *"Sorry, we're not home"* greeting. Now they answer:

"Hello. Only we could make this announcement. The Fingers are not on hand."

I wonder why doctors haven't used the answering machine more creatively. They could "examine" you right on the phone.

"Hello. You've reached the office of Dr. Shmidler, dermatology and cosmetic surgery. Please make a selection from the following menu at any time:

If you are in pain, press 1.

If you are in agony, press 2.

If you are pealing or flaking, press 3.

If you are oozing, press 4.

If you have pimples, squeeze 5.

If you are itching, scratch 6.

If you are black and blue, smack 7.

If you have a suspicious looking rash above the waistline, press 8.

If you have a suspicious looking rash below the waistline, first put on a glove, then press 9.

If you are calling about a face lift, eye job, cheek or chin implants, breast enlargement or reduction, press 0 and a doctor will be with you in 30 seconds.

Hey, if any of you out there are named, Lite or Light, how about this for a message:

"Hello. Sorry, the lights are out."

P.

The telephone companies must be cleaning up. Everybody, everywhere is talking on a cell phone. They're yaking away at airports and movies..... on every street corner.....in restaurants and all over the malls. And now they've made it even easier to yakety yak anywhere you are. Now you don't even have to hold a phone. Have you seen these things growing out of people's ears. This is weird. You see a guy walking toward you talking to himself. And he's yelling. No, screaming. He's angry. At what? At who? He's alone. This guy is nuts. A loony. I'd better cross the street. Get out of his way. Then you see the growth in his ear. Weirdo.

But the telephone companies can't cash in on the most frequent call of all. The call we all get. The caller that keeps calling us.....many times in the middle of the night. Many times more than once. I refer to that moment when Mother Nature calls. Or as a poet once put it....."*When You Gotta Go.....You Gotta Go.*"

I think men get this call more often than women. It's a prostate thing. Guys, this is a call you can't hang up on or call back. This is a call you can't even put on hold. This is a call you must answer immediately. This is that panicky moment when your brain calls your bladder..... **"A.S.A.P.P......As Soon As Possible Pee."**

By all means, take that "A.S.A.P.P." very seriously. The clock is ticking. You can go from "i gotta go"— to "I Gotta Go"— to **"I GOTTA GO!!!,"** in the zip of a zipper! This could turn into a *Depends* moment at any moment. But at this moment, there is another element as important as speed. You gotta know where you can go when you gotta go and you're not home. Yes, you have to know your way around the "P" circuit. Where are the good pit stops? Who will welcome you and who will not? Wise men know. I've made a study. I'll give you a quick "P" tour.

Banks. They don't like strangers. Their facility is only for customers putting in or taking out. You're letting out.

Restaurants. The hostess will stop you. Like the banks, their facility is for their customers use only. I once bought a bowl of soup just to qualify. That's how desperate I was.

Department Stores. I give them a perfect "P" rating. Nobody knows what you're there for. But it can be hard to find the "P" room. And it can be a long walk. Why is it, no matter where you walk into a department store, the rest room is always at the other end of the place? Even worse, there could be an escalator ride between you and relief. And let me tell you, if you're getting frantic "A.S.A.P.P." calls, the last place you want to be is stuck on an escalator doing .01 mph, trapped behind a wide body. I hope you got strong thighs!

Book Stores. Great. Everybody's got their nose in a book. They don't even know you came, you went, you left.

Hotels. You can't beat them for a pit stop. Nobody asks any questions. They don't know who you are. But try to avoid the fancy places. You may run into a guy who hands you a towel and has a plate full of dollar bills in plain view. But then again, at a time like this, a buck may be a bargain.

Gas Stations. This is the standard pit stop but not the most inviting. I always feel funny asking the guy for the key and then leaving without buying any gas. So I usually buy a few guilty gallons. But with the price of gas today, and as often as I gotta go, now I just pee and flee.

Oops, gotta go. My bladder is ringing.

411

I'm not a cell phone person. I'm just not, "Mr. Modern." I don't know how I survived for so long without out that little marvel hooked up to my belt. I never had a cell phone for two reasons: 1) Nobody ever calls me. 2) I never call anybody. I was very happy. I didn't have Tiger's problems.

Well, I'm no longer a hold out. No longer am I facing life phone-less. I now have a cell phone. Yes , just like you, I now ring. And vibrate. I'm hooked up. But what has it gotten me.

It's just another number to remember. And I can't do any tricks with my phone like a lot of guys show off. I can't text on it. I can't look at pictures of my kids on it because I can't take pictures of my kids on it. I can't get stock prices or movie times or read a newspaper on it. I can only do 2 cell phone things. I can make a call and I can answer a call. I'm not even that good on the latter. If you call me and leave a message, chances are better than 50-50, in my fumbling to retrieve it, I'll erase it.

But there's a bigger problem. I can't get your message if I can't find my cell phone. My answering message says it all— *"Hi, please leave your name and number. I'll call you back as soon as I find my cell phone."* As I write this, it's been missing.....for 3 days.* I can never remember where I leave it. Who needs this? I have enough to forget.

But I am not a total dialing dodo head. I can do a terrific trick on my cell phone. I've been deliberating on whether or not to tell you this story. I think it ages me. But know this, I am sharp and keen of mind despite what happened to me and my cell phone on this particular day.

I was out driving when I stopped to perform a bit of cellular magic. I was expecting an important call at home. I would call my home phone on my cell and get my messages off my answering machine. Right from my car! Is that 21st Century! Is that Wow!

I took out my cell and started dialing my number. After 3 numbers, I stopped. Wait a minute.....that's not my number. I tried again. Again it wasn't my number. I tried a few more times. No luck. I couldn't remember my number. Understand, I wasn't calling an airline or my lawyer or a restaurant. I was calling my headquarters, my home..... my base of operations. I was calling *MYSELF!* (And you should have heard what I was calling myself!)

I needed a rest. I took off a minute or two and didn't think about it. The rest didn't help. I was still clueless and numberless. At that point, I did what you would have done. No, I didn't give up. No, I didn't wait till I got home. Are you sitting down? I called information. (Tell me you would have called information, too.)

I don't know if you can imagine how stupid and brainless I felt giving the information operator my name and address. But I was about to feel even more stupid. Would you believe it, I started disguising my voice so she wouldn't know it was me asking for me. How ridiculous! How could she know?

This very disturbing incident has taught me a very valuable lesson. I can never have an unlisted number.

*Update: I had to buy a new phone. I kept my unforgettable number.

**Up-Update: As soon as I bought the new phone, I found the lost one.

Home Suite Home

THE #1#

It's amazing how many numbers we carry around in our heads.....and know cold! Telephone numbers.....fax numbers.....addresses and zip codes.....not only yours, but your kids. Don't forget their birthdays either. And as for your social security number.....you could give it to me in a flash. Your safe combination? Never have to look it up. Of course you know your cholesterol number. Bet you even know your good HDL's and your bad HDL's.

I'm here today to tell you to forget all those numbers. They're just cluttering your mind. Make room for the only number you have to know.....and remember.....and never forget. Probably the most important number in your life. Ladies and gentlemen, if you can remember only one number, remember the number.....YOUR SQUARE FOOTAGE!

Face it folks, in this day and age, you are your square footage. Some people are quiet about it but others advertise it. They can't wait to tell you. They give it to you even though you never asked for it. Take "Mr. Subtlety." He always finds a way to slip his square footage into the conversation. You're out playing golf with this guy who just moved into the neighborhood. You ask him:

"How are you enjoying the area?"

"Who's has time to enjoy. You know what it's like moving into 12,000 square feet?"

Friends, you just got "squared" and you never saw it coming. You know this man for maybe an hour. You never met his wife.....if he has one. You know nothing about his kids.....if he has any. You don't know his background or his business.....but he sure made it his business to give you his square footage.

Then there's the guy I call the "Great Approximater."

"I don't know how much space I've got. I'd guess between 4500 and 5,000 square feet."

This guy's got four thousand five hundred and <u>ONE</u> square foot..... and not one foot more.

Now, I'm sure you've run into the guy who lets you know how rich he <u>used</u> to be.

"We sold our house up north and moved down here. You know what it's like trying to fit 14,000 square feet of stuff into 4,000?"

Have you ever met the guy who gives you coming attractions? As he puts it....."I've got a nice comfortable 7,000 square feet. Don't ask me why I'm putting on a 5,000 foot addition." So you could tell me you're going to have 12,000 feet.

And bless the soul who lives a contented existence. Listen to a man satisfied with his lot in life. (Waterview?) "I love my house. The only problem is it's too big. I don't need 16,000 square feet. I could be very happy in 10,000." Ah, a man of simple needs and wants.

My favorite is the guy who's living on borrowed square footage. You ask him where he lives.

"You've probably passed my place. You know that big house on the corner of Bird Dr.? Sits there like a castle. 5 car garage. Indoor, outdoor pool. Solarium, tennis court and putting green. I'm 2 houses down from that."

Of course a lot of these guys are including porches and patios and big roof overhangs.....even the cement platform for their garbage cans. So next time you get "squared," just ask how many feet they've got <u>under air</u>.

That'll get rid of a lotta hot air.

I NEED A FIX

I don't know if it's the southern climate or just my lousy luck, but I am constantly sitting around waiting for a repairman to come and fix my latest possession to break down. This is my job in life. It's not only time consuming and money consuming.....it's boring!

What's even worse, it's depressing and maddening. Every workman walks in, looks at the problem and then gives me the same depressing spiel. Example: my hot water heater isn't working right. Does the plumber come in and fix it quietly? He can't! He stands there looking at my heater, shaking his head—

"I don't know who installed this heater, Mr. Bushell, but he didn't know what he was doing. (Boy do I feel stupid and taken advantage of.) Look for yourself.....he never hooked up the pressure line into the gravity pump. (I can't believe I didn't see that.) I hope this guy didn't do any other plumbing in your house."

I'm embarrassed to say he did. Like the whole house! I was going to ask this guy to also look at the sink in the laundry room but I'm afraid he'll figure out the same guy who did the hot water heater, did the sink. I'm feeling like such a dumb-dumb already, I can't take any more.

And this is how it goes every time I need a fix.

The painter....."Whoever did this paint job didn't give it a second spackle coat. That's why you have cracks. If you shelled out for 2 coats, you didn't get it." I was robbed again!

The electrician—"Whoever installed these fixtures could have burned your house down with this wiring." Forget stupid! I'm a threat to my family.....my neighbors.....the whole area!

The air conditioning guy—"Your house is always freezing because somebody sold you a ton of air conditioning you don't need. (Ripped off again! I'm a pushover! A sucker!)

My new gardner stops by—"Mr. Bushell, your Hookaloosa Palm is dying."

"Oh no, Reggie, not my Hookaloosa!

"It's a shame, Mr. Bushell, they're magnificent."

"I don't want to sound stupid, Reggie, but which one is my Hookalosa Palm?"

"The dried up, droopy one over there. It's a very expensive specimen. I don't want to ask you how much you paid for it. (Raked over by the gardener. That makes me feel real good.)

I sense where this conversation is going but my masochistic side must ask the question, "What's the problem, Reggie?"

"Whoever you hired to plant it is the problem. The guy put it in the sun. Hookaloosas hate the sun. You can see the sun is just strangling the life out of that poor palm." (This guy is making me feel like a killer.) Any gardener who ever planted anything, knows Hookaloosas love shade.

Leave it to me to find a plumber who can't hook up a heater—a painter who short changes me on spackle—an air conditioning guy who freezes me out—and now on top of all that, I gotta find the only gardener around who's a Hookaloosa loser!

I'm telling you all this because tomorrow I've got the roofer coming. His company did my roof 19 years ago. I don't know if he remembers. I purposely picked him because if he says one word—I'm ready!

MOVE OVER NEWTON

This is for all you pool owners. I don't know which category you belong in.

A) You bought a resale and it came with a pool. You inherited yours.

B) You built a brand new home and foolishly decided to build it with a pool.

I say foolishly because you now realize what a financial drain your hole in the ground is. Especially foolish because you never go in. You're not a swimmer. You're not even a dunker.....or a wader.....or a treader of water.....or a dangler of feet.....or a big toe tester.....or a floater on vinyl. You're strictly a chaiser. Let me put it this way.....do you even own a bathing suit? And if you do, ladies.....would you ever appear in it?

So you never go in your pool. But it's so nice to just lounge around poolside and relax. Except you never go out. It's too hot. It's too buggy. It's too humid. It's too sunny. It's too windy. I'm too busy. I'm too tired. I've got too much to do. You always have a "Too" for not pooling it.

But there are times.....the only times.....when your pool is filled with frolicking bodies. Your grandchildren come down and can't wait to jump into your hole in the ground. These moments are worth the whole cost of the pool. Until you get the heating bill. Yes, maintaining a pool is a dive into big bucks. Keeping those cool, glistening waters, clean and perfectly pH balanced, takes a lot of M&M.....maintenance and money.

And of course there is that universal pool owner's dread.....leaks! If you own a pool, your pool has a leak.....has had a leak.....or will have a leak. It's inevitable. I had a leak for years. I was out there every few days adding water to my pool. I finally called a pool company to fix my leak.

They wanted to dig up the patio to find the leak. Dig up my patio? Are you crazy? I'd sooner fill in the pool. Then one day genius hit me like it hit Newton. It was just another annoying day of me out there "watering" the pool. I was watching the water flow in through a spout in the deep end. I remember the moment. It was inspirational! Standing there, I had a poolside epiphany. In that moment, I knew how Newton must have felt under the apple tree. The solution to my leak was so simple:

Instead of the water flowing in, suppose it was just trickling in. Aha! Suppose I let the trickle just keep trickling.

Better yet.....suppose I never turned off the trickle! Could I lick the leak with a trickle? The trick'll be to perfectly balance the trickle leaking out with the trickle trickling in. If I could pull off that little trickle trick, the leak'll be licked. (Pure Cole Porter!)

Yes, my pool owning friends with a leak, listen carefully—THE TRICK IS IN THE TRICKLE!

So I fiddled with the trickle. I got it so the water was trickling in at the same rate it was trickling out. It was a trickle tie! A standoff! Thanks to that little trickle, I was no longer in a pickle.....and it didn't cost me an extra nickel!

Friends, come on over and see my trickle. You'll get a tickle out of my trickle.

The caterers are not happy.

Cancel the little franks.

ARE THEY MARRIED... OR "MARRIED"?

Life used to be so much simpler. Take the institution of marriage. Men and women used to be married or single. Married couples had a real partnership. One partner carried the X chromosome and the other carried the Y.

Now we have same sex marriages. They are filled with love and devotion but they sure screw up the chromosome arrangement. On the other hand, it sure makes for a gay old time.

Now we also have non-marriage "marriages." It's happening every day. Older woman meets older man. Woman likes man. Man likes woman. For whatever reason, very often financial, neither wants to get married. So woman dubs man her, "Significant Other".....or vice versa. A simple dubbing is all it takes. "Love and marriage" is for the young at heart. But for the older hearts, "Significant Other" is a match made in heaven.

"Significant Other".....what a strange phrase. Obviously, you have not found your "adored other." You're only committing to "significant." But that leaves room. One day should you find that adored one, is it, "Adios, Significant Other?"

Indeed, where exactly does "significant" fit into the lexicon of love? I guess it instantly makes all other suitors insignificant. Although it's a level of feeling below infatuation or adoration, it is still strong enough and heartfelt enough, for the "significant other" to move right in.

From the outside looking in, there's really no significant difference between marrieds and significant others. But getting married is far more complicated than getting "othered." Getting "othered" requires no City Hall visit or blood test or license. And since there is no official ceremony or celebration, there's no need for a preacher man to utter those hallowed words, "I now pronounce you Significant Others." Yes, married's "tie the knot" but significant others prefer "no strings attached." How simple. No prenup!

Nor is there any need for a caterer. Forget the hors d'oeuvres! (I'll miss the little hot dogs!) Forget the dinners! And you don't have to buy drinks for a load of freeloading relatives you haven't seen in ages. It's so simple. No band or florist or photographer needed. And no diamond ring, guys. Maybe a piece of jewelry to mark the occasion. The only thing you need to become Significant Others....is an "other."

How then does one graduate from insignificant to significant? I suppose it's like a marriage proposal: "Darling, I have very significant feelings for you. Will you become my significant other? Will you love, honor and obey, til the kids do us part?"

And how do significant others celebrate their anniversaries? Are there Hallmark cards especially for them? If there aren't, you're missing a significant boat here, Hallmark. Maybe they raise their glasses in a champagne toast, "Darling, here's to our fifth Significant Other anniversary". (Very clumsy wording on the anniversary cake.) And what romantic anniversary song shall they dance to? Andrew Lloyd Webber hasn't written a "Significant Other" love song yet.

All in all, "Significants" do not get to enjoy the same hoopla and excitement that newlyweds do. But the day may come when *The New York Times* carries their news, too:

"Zelda Frompkin and Valdez Wister become Significant Others. The "othering" took place February 3, at 2 a.m., in Ms. Frompkin's bedroom."

Significant news.

MY WIFE'S COMING BACK A SECOND WIFE

Today there is a whole new language of love. An older married man becomes single. He meets a much younger lady. Beautiful. Shapely. Sexy. She lights a fire in his innards. (You know which innard.) He displays her on his arm like a Renoir. At his age, there is no time for a long courtship. He snatches her for his wife.....his "Trophy Wife"! Ahhh, the "Trophy Wife".....the kind of woman every man dreams of.....but few can afford.

Just a few notches below "Trophy Wives," there are the "envied second wives".....envied because they seem to sit on a higher throne than the first wife. They are treated to a more regal lifestyle.....a more pampered existence.....and most enviable of all, they always appear more bedecked and bejeweled than Mrs. #1. Recently, a local country club passed a rule to ease this second wife syndrome:

"Any second wife attending a club function may wear a maximum 15.5 karats. This includes her neck, fingers, wrists, ear lobes and any baubles dangling in her cleavage or nestled in her navel."

In no time, this new rule claimed it's first violator. A second wife was brought before the grievance committee for exceeding the 15.5 limit at a club dance. The prosecution described her glitter, gem by dazzling gem. There was no part of her left unbedecked. It seemed an open and shut case. But the defense had an answer.

Yes, she was dazzling but her dazzle was all faux! And faux has no karats. The 15.5 rule did not apply. The defense was brilliant. The prosecution was stunned. They asked for a recess to regroup.

When the hearing resumed, the prosecution was ready. They showed a widely read handbook, considered the Bible for second wives. There was a special section entitled: "Going On A Bling-Bling Fling." It stated, "Second wives shall not wear faux jewelry. Second wives say, "Foo on faux!""

The defense had no answer. The lady was found guilty.

The grievance committee meted out unusual punishment. They did not ban her from using the club for a period of time, as is usually the case. No, they handed out even harsher punishment. They allowed her full use of the club, but for two weeks, she was not allowed to wear any jewelry while at the club. None!

"That's not a sentence.....that's torture," complained other envied second wives. But their feelings were ameliorated when the sentenced lady was seen retrieving her golf ball from a lake. The handbook clearly states, "Second wives do not retrieve golf balls. You wet it—forget it!" She was no longer a card carrying second wife.

Throughout this ordeal, her husband was caring, considerate and concerned. When the ordeal was finally over, he thought he would lift her spirits and cheer her heart. He got her.....you guessed it.....a new little bling-bling thing. Which I understand.....all by itself.....exceeds the 15.5 limit.

Ain't love grand.

~~Frittered~~
~~Thrown out~~
~~Squandered~~
~~Blown~~
~~Wasted~~

**Oh, the money I've ~~spent~~
on golf and bridge lessons**

MAYBE, IF YOU LIVE TO 100... MAYBE

Do you play golf? I do.

Are you good? I'm not.

I know I sound a bit negative but it hasn't always been that way. Actually, I started playing golf with great hope and expectations. And yes, with great joy, too. As the pars and very occasional birdies started creeping into my game, I grew even more optimistic. So much so in fact, I let myself believe I was made for this game. I even let myself believe that one day I would achieve the greatest feat in all of golfdom. One day I was going to shoot my age.

I didn't know which age but I knew just how I would react. I would frame the scorecard. Bronze the ball! Throw a party! What a dreamer!

Well, the dream didn't last long. I realized early on they would never make golf clubs good enough nor would I ever live long enough to achieve this feat.

But I'm a goal oriented kind of person. I need something to shoot for. So I lowered my expectations. I decided to stay within my capabilities.

If I can't shoot my age.....I'll shoot my temperature.

Things went well. I was more relaxed. My grip loosened. My tempo slowed. I loved golf again. I was achieving my goal.

But then I noticed a change. Slight at first but impossible to ignore. My scores were inching up. My goal was in danger. Oh, I was still shooting my temperature.....but with the flu!

Again, I had to adjust my thinking. I lowered my sights. I faced reality. Forget my temperature. I would now shoot my blood pressure.

It's going pretty well now but there are times on the course, when I'm butchering a hole, I can feel my blood pressure rising. But not as fast as my score.

As I ponder this further deterioration, I wonder.....is it possible? Can it be? One day could I.....shoot my cholesterol?????

BRIDGE TAKES A TOLL

I always thought golf was the hardest game of all. Move over golf. Meet bridge. Bridge is 3-4 hours of tension, hand-after-hand combat and mind boggling concentration, all while you're locked in a stress-drenched room, stuck sedentary in a chair and playing against team after team of serious, somber faced enemies who are out to destroy you.

Yes, golf is competition.....but bridge is war!

You will never get a tan playing bridge. (You'll probably get paler!) You will never hear a joke. Rarely will you ever see a smile. Grim rules. Bridge is very sanitary. Nobody shakes hands. You will never hear the words, "Good luck" or "Nice play" from your opponents.

Bridge is more like a religion than a game and its worshipers, the Bridgees, are devout followers. They talk bridge on the golf course..... waiting for the movie to start.....in the gym.....at dinner. Yes, golfers will often replay a hole or two over dinner, but Bridgees will replay hands through cocktails and well into the appetizer. If your having dinner with some Bridgees, bring a book!

Here are some Bridge no-no's so you're not accused of sending secret signals to your partner. Don't scratch yourself no matter how bad you itch.....don't change the volume of your voice.....speak in a monotone.....don't cough or clear your throat or hiccup.....don't blink out of rhythm.....sit very still.....don't shift cheeks too often.....don't make any sudden or abrupt movements. Just sit motionless, expressionless and lifeless.....like a lump. (If you have a nervous tic, don't take up bridge.)

The competition in Bridge is so intense and combative, there must always be a "cop" on the premises. This is the enforcer, who is euphemistically called, the "Director." When one suspects wrong doing, one merely raises their hand and calls out, "DIRECTOR!" This is Bridge's version of 911. This sets the wheels of justice in motion.

The Director rushes to the scene to adjudicate the issue and penalize if necessary. Of course, this whole matter is so trivial, it wouldn't even be heard in Small Claims Court. But for Bridgees, this is the Supreme Court!

Bridge demands a good memory. How many trump are out.....who bid the diamonds.....how many clubs have been played? Forget it! You probably can't even remember the names of the other people at your table. Thank, God, you don't have to. Just call them by their Bridge-given names.....North, East, South and West.

Now, the big thing in bridge is conventions. You and your partner take endless lessons to learn the hottest new ones. One day, the bidding calls for one of your hot new conventions. Without hesitation, your partner bids it and you immediately say, "Alert."

HOLD IT! STOP THE PRESSES!!!

Now get this.....the rules say you have to "alert" the opponents that you are doing something unusual. I guess that's the same in football when the quarterback has to alert the defense there's a trick play coming. (Who wrote this rule?)

Your opponents never heard this bid. Now get this.....the rules further state, your opponents.....YOUR SWORN ENEMIES!!!.....can ask you, "What did your partner mean by that bid?" You have no choice. It's tell them or....."DIRECTOR!" You are fit to be tied. So you tell them, "Listen, I paid $100 to learn this convention. Give me fifty bucks and I'll tell you what it means."

Settle for 25!

Sometimes it's hard to find the **humor**

Of all the medical exams and tests we are subjected to.....the jabs and poking.....the looking down you.....the looking up you.....the needles and bloodletting.....the drilling and filling.....for me, there is one procedure that is the most fearful. Amazingly enough, it doesn't hurt. This does not involve pain. This procedure involves far worse—rigid, tight, suffocating enclosure. Welcome to the MRI.

I'm not talking about those easy-to-take, open MRI's. I'm talking the real thing.....the enclosed MRI. You know what MRI stands for....."Meager Room Inside." Better yet....."Measly Room Inside." I think this machine was invented by an anorexic scientist.

To lie in an MRI is to know how a torpedo feels just before it is fired. A piece of advice. Don't open your eyes. The view is terrifying. The top of the machine is just inches from your nose. (If you've got a big shnoz, duck!) If you're claustrophobic you will begin to sweat, palpitate, hyperventilate and cringe. And that's before you even get in the machine. That's just from looking at it.

My wife is very claustrophobic. She starts palpitating 3 or 4 days before her appointment. She can't get in the machine without a couple of valiums and me, sitting in the room with her, rubbing her feet and talking her through it. She is so terrified of this machine, she won't even read this column.

Just how tight is it inside an MRI? Let me paint you a picture. Lying in an MRI, you are in the same boat as King Tut.....or should I say, the same sarcophagus? Forget enclosed. You are entombed! The good news? Tut was in for a couple of centuries. You're out in 30 minutes.

But space is not the only hardship you must endure. Once the test begins, you must stay absolutely motionless. In other words—make like Tut. Lie there at attention with your arms pressed against your sides. Don't move.....or wiggle.....or squirm.....or scratch.....or cough..... or even breath heavy. Easy for Tut. Not for you. To help keep you still, they strap you in which only heightens the fear and terror. Of course, Tut didn't need a strap. He was wiggleless.

And to make sure you don't get a panic attack, they blindfold you so you won't see where you are. This is for the peekers.....people who can't keep their eyes shut. Keeping Tut shut was no problem. So instead of a blindfold, they gave him a beautiful 24k gold mask. (His to keep.) I guess times were better then.

Not only are you strapped in and blindfolded, they also give you ear plugs. Why the ear plugs? Because once started, the machine assaults your hearing with a loud, deafening, discordant cacophony of banging, clanging magnets. It's like something from a bad acid rock band. Some MRI places offer you headphones instead of ear plugs. You can drown out the magnets with Sinatra or Streisand or Broadway. One time, I clamped on my headphones and the first song up was.....you wouldn't believe it....."Don't Fence Me In."

I have a plea for all you MRI makers. Could you start thinking big? Could you start thinking—More Room Inside!

WE'LL HAVE TO CONDO THE WHITE HOUSE

Could our world ever face more daunting, more perilous problems than we face today? I think things could get worse. I can see a world where terror reigns. Nobody flies anymore. You no longer go through a body scan. You now go through a locker room.

Gas is un-buyable. We are over OPEC's barrel. Immigration is flowing like a gusher. *McDonalds* and *Taco Bell* have opened up right on the border to feed all the hungry hikers coming across. Iran is working on on H-Bomb. Even little Guatemala is enriching uranium.

The economy? There is no more exchange rate. Nobody wants to exchange for dollars. Health care is hemorrhaging. The future has never been bleaker. All this as a Presidential election nears.

The President seems aged and beaten, when he/she addresses the nation from the Oval Office. Emotionally drained and teary eyed, he/she quotes the battered and beaten boxer, Roberto Duran, and declares, "No mas. No mas. I will not run again."

The country is shocked and anxiously waits for young, new leaders to declare their candidacy. But nobody throws their hat in the ring. Not a single red or blue stater. And then *The New York Times* headlines the unthinkable, the impossible.....a constitutional calamity:

NOBODY WANTS TO BE PRESIDENT

The ripples from this crisis are immediate and far reaching. Conventions are canceled. Thousands of professional conventioneers have to put away their noisemakers and stupid hats. Protesters by the thousands are left picketless. About 100,000 balloons lie in a warehouse—unblown. Confetti makers stop shredding. Sign makers become resigned. Debates are canceled. Presidential speech writers are speechless. The Secret Service finds itself off guard.

Fears grow over possible mold in the oval office. Air Force One will have to be sold. (To Donald, no doubt.) Americans wonder if they will ever again hear the stirring strains of, *"Hail To The Chief."* And who will meet, greet and fete visiting foreign dignitaries? Even more distressing, how will we know the state of the union.....without a "State of the Union?"

Amidst all this confusion and consternation, Al Gore sounds a positive note. He reminds the nation that Global Warming will be spared a whole lot of hot air.

But something must be done. The country looks to Congress to act. Unaccustomed as they are to acting, they debate, argue and accuse. Finally, they come together and devise a plan. They will solve this problem as they solve every problem.....with money.

They will go to a leading executive placement firm.....no, better yet, they will go to a leading sports agent to design a blockbuster pay package the likes of which only a sports agent could conceive. He comes up with a package that would make the most revered sports icon or greediest corporate CEO feel vastly underpaid, under perked and under appreciated.

In addition to huge salary increases, lifetime expense accounts, a health plan that even covers the Presidential dog and unlimited use of Air Force One (to tempt Nancy of the House), there is a provision that makes George Steinbrenner look like Scrooge. As an annual bonus, the President will be paid a percentage of the Gross National Product, geared to the GNP's performance during their term. Who else but a sports agent could dream on such a scale?

And now, back to now. I don't know if a scenario like this will ever come to pass. Hopefully, we will always have plenty of egos eager to run. But if one day nobody wants the job, I know one thing.....don't come to me.

I've already turned down President of my condo.

Two old ladies chatting...

Edith,
It's not how old you are.
It's how old you
feel.

I'll
have to ask,
Harold, how old
I feel.

WHAT'S "WHAT'S-HIS-NAME'S" NAME?

Do you know which word has been spoken more often than any other? It's our little friend, "The". Do you know which word has just replaced "The" as the most spoken? I know what you're thinking but this is a clean word. The new holder of the "Most Spoken Word" title is.....may I have a drum roll, please.....our even littler friend, "Uh".

Webster defines "Uh" as an *"expression of hesitation."* But there's much more to "Uh" than that. With your indulgence, Mr. W., allow me to define it....."Uh" *is a word used to stall and buy time when you can't remember the name of the person, place or thing you're trying to recall. Example....."I saw this great movie. It was called.....uh.....uh.....it was about a dog called.....uh.....uh....."*

Some say "Uh" is a "phfumfer".....a kind of stutter or stammer when you can't get the words out. Indeed "Uh" can sound like one is phumfering. "Uh-ing" comes on with age like arthritis and cataracts. Its rapidly growing usage is directly related to our aging population. A research group recently reported that the over 60 crowd is 82% more likely to "Uh" their way through life than the under 60's.

"Uh" is rarely spoken singly but rather in a series of 3 or 4 quick repetitions, much like a broken record repeating itself. "Uh" is usually accompanied by short snaps of the finger as though the speaker was trying to jog their memory.....a kind of manual shock therapy. There is no scientific evidence that snapping helps.

"Uh" is contagious. If you're talking with a group and start "Uh-ing" over a forgotten word, then others in the group, who know the word but can't think of it either, may also start "Uhing" and snapping their fingers in support of you. A casual passerby may wonder what is going on with these people? This choral "Uh-ing" really ups its usage.

If all this "Uhing" and finger snapping can only bring the word to the tip of the tongue, and no further, the speaker may finally end his "Uh-ing" with an, "I give up" shrug. But shrugs don't end sentences. Periods do and no respectable period would be caught dead appearing after, "Uh". Problem is, how do we end this continuous stream of phfumfered "Uhs" and get out of this sentence we're trapped in.

Solution. We cap it off with words of our own invention.....words coined by a phfumfering people who can't remember. I call these words "Uh" enders. They bring the sentence to an end. Example:

"The engine stalled because they didn't oil the.....uh.....uh.....you know.....the.....uh.....uh.....the.....uh whatchamacallit"

Whatchamacallit! Sheer phonetic genius. It says nothing, and yet, says it all. And just as expressive, we have whatchamacallit's cousin, whosamawhatsis.....as in, "Good thing I picked up that, uh.....uh..... whosamawhatsis for the sink today.

WHAT-CHA-MA-CALL-IT! WHO-SA-MA-WHAT-SIS! What a lyrical, syncopated stretch of syllables strung together like a set of South Sea pearls? They glide over your tongue as smooth as Fred Astaire's feet over a ballroom floor.

And how about when you can't remember a person's name. "We played golf with.....uh.....you know the guy from Chicago.....uh—uh— WHATSHISNAME." Or did you play with, WHATSHISFACE? What's the difference? It's the same guy!

Lucky for us, we've got our own little, looney language. We couldn't converse or communicate without our cockamamie vocabulary (It's spelled right. I looked it up).

CANDLE POWER

Like all of us, you began with one candle. Of course you were too young to appreciate what all the fuss was about. I speak of that first birthday.....certainly a milestone for your parents, if not for you. And as you grew older and the candlepower grew greater, the celebrations grew more joyous.....specially when you hit those "milestones."

Who could forget #18? You could vote. You could drink. And just three years later at 21, many of us had a college degree, a resume and hopefully, our first real job. Then there was the 30 year milestone. You celebrated with a mate and maybe a kid or two. You went from "I" to "We". And 10 years later, at 40, the younger generation started calling you, "Mr." The fiftieth was a bit unsettling. When your parents turned 50, you thought they were ancient. And now you're ancient.

I've clicked off all those milestones including the big "6". And just recently I celebrated the next one. I threw a little party. My wife and I invited some friends.....all contemporaries.....and I toasted the event.

"Thank you all for coming tonight. I must say, I feel young. I'm struck by the difference between tonight and the night I celebrated my fiftieth. I remember I came to that one right from the office. To-night, I came right from my nap. Also, back then I didn't have to talk as loud as I'm talking tonight. And I didn't have to wear glasses to read my speech. In fact, I didn't have to read it. I could remember it. Remember when we could remember?

But, guys, I will say you are an impressive crowd for your age. When it comes to knees and hips, we've got a lot of original equipment here tonight. And as I look around, all men are present and accounted for. There's not a single guy in the men's room.

But time has left its mark and made some big changes in us. Welcome to Stentville! Yes, we have a lot of stents in the crowd tonight. Twenty five years ago, who'd a thunk one day the road to wellness..... the road to long life.....the road to the fountain of youth, would run through the groin. Today the groin is a lifeline. Back then, the groin was something athletes were always pulling.

Not only do we have stents here tonight, we have quite a few bypasses. Our blood flows in, out, around and through detours and bypasses like traffic through construction on the Turnpike. Our red and white blood cells must be totally lost and confused. If you listen real close, you can hear them talking.....

'Hey, Red, aren't we supposed to go left here?'

'Relax, Whitey, we can't go left. It's blocked.'

'I don't remember this stretch.'

'We used to take it down the leg.'

'So what's it doing up here?'

'They designed a whole new layout, Whitey.'

'Where are we headed, Red?'

'We're headed for a shot in the arm, a kick in the butt, a boost in the behind—we're headed for the Big Pumping Station.'

'Are you sure, Red? Cause I'm tired. I really need a push.'

'Just look ahead, Whitey. What do you see? Coming right up. Just a heart beat away. It's Aorta Avenue! The Great Red Way.'

So, friends, my message is simple. Listen to Red and Whitey. If you want to get to your next milestone, keep Aorta Ave. clear of any STOP signs."

Good advice, folks. Take it to heart!

Star Gazing

JFK/LAX

When I was still a working adman, I did a lot of flying. My most frequent destination was Los Angeles. I shot a lot of commercials out there in "La La" Land.

Because my flying was on business, I had the pleasure of sitting up front with all the big expense account honchos. The N.Y./L.A. run was a star studded experience. I found myself flying with the likes of Paul Newman, Dolly Parton, Bette Middler, Lucy and Desi. But enough name dropping.

Of all the stars I flew with, there is one flight that stands out. It was an unforgettable experience for me—and I'd like to think, for the star, too. This is a true story. It happened 35,000 feet over somewhere between JFK and LAX.

We were in the air for about two hours when I wended my way up front for a pit stop. I didn't know it at the time, but Mother Nature had far more exciting plans for me than just another tinkle. On the way back to my seat, I noticed a gentleman seated on the aisle about two rows ahead. I thought to myself, "This guy could be Gregory Peck's double." A few steps further, I <u>screamed</u> to myself, "IT <u>IS</u> GREGORY PECK. IT'S HIM!"

Please understand, I am not one of those star struck fliers. But Gregory Peck was not just a star. He was a Galaxy! He exuded such class and elegance, dressed in a beautiful gray suit, with the perfect matching tie. Me? The beautiful jacket and tie would have been off and shoved into the bin above before I even sat down. Not Mr. Peck! An equally elegant lady was seated next to him. Mrs. Peck, no doubt.

I had every intention of going directly back to my seat but as I passed him, I had one of my crazy thoughts. Being impetuous, I never considered the consequences. I stopped and patted him on the shoulder. He looked up from the book he was reading, peered at me over the rim of his glasses and in that grand, stentorian, "To-Kill-A-Mockingbird" baritone, he uttered,

"Yes?"

It was only a syllable but a syllable never sounded so Godly.

"Excuse the interruption, Mr. Peck, my name is, Gordon Bushell."

"Yes?" It was an even grander "Yes" than his first.

So there I stood, face to face with Gregory Peck. I thought to myself, "All right, Bushell, go ahead and make a fool of yourself."

"As I passed your seat, Mr. Peck, an idea occurred to me."

"Yes?"

"Do you realize, Mr. Peck, that between us.....we are a "BUSHEL AND A PECK?"

I held my breath. Would he have me deported to economy class? Surprise! He laughed. No it was more of a roar. He slapped his thigh in delight. He introduced me to his wife. I repeated it for her. After all, she and I were also a, "Bushel and a Peck". She roared. Elegantly.

I wanted to get on the PA system and tell the whole plane, "Ladies and gentlemen, did you know you're flying with a, "Bushel and a Peck?" He shook my hand. We chatted for awhile, enjoying our linguistic link. Yes, 35,000 feet up, we bonded.

Greg and I.

MY BRUSH WITH FAME

For many people, the advertising business is an offshoot, a kissin' cousin of Show Biz. They attach a certain glamor and glitz to Madison Ave.. Lights.....action.....camera! It could be a movie or a commercial. Working as an adman, I can recall a memorable time when I found myself with one foot in Hollywood and the other on Mad. Ave..

I had written a spot for a relatively new product called, Ultra Brite toothpaste. It had been introduced as the "Sex Appeal" toothpaste. Back then, "sex appeal" were two daring words for prime time TV. Fortunately, the censors let it run. My how things have changed. Do we have any censors censoring anything any more?

Ultra Brite was the toothpaste for people more interested in getting a Saturday night date than avoiding cavities. To speak to that sexually driven hunk of the population.....and it was a hunk.....I wrote a campaign that said, "Mother Never Told Me About Ultra Brite." (Whose mother didn't play censor?)

The idea was simple. A pretty, young lady would say, "Mother always told me to sit up straight.....eat all your vegetables.....and go to sleep early. But Mother never told me about Ultra Brite."

I envisioned those words being spoken by a beautiful, wholesome young lady, probably blonde, sitting in a lush, verdant countryside, bathed in gleaming sunlight. Of course she had to have a smile worthy of the sex appeal toothpaste. And she had to be able to deliver the words in the coy and playful style I heard in my head. So where do you find beautiful, young blondes, lush countryside and golden sunlight?

L.A.! So there I sat in Hollywood, in the director's office, casting for beautiful young ladies. One after another they came in with their big proof books. Funny, when they walk in, they're pretty. But when you look at their pictures, they're gorgeous. The lens does wonders for some people. After 20 minutes of casting, I thought we had some contenders. Well, Gordon, you ain't seen nothin' yet!

The door opened and into the room walked this spectacular, young lady. As they say in Hollywood, she was B&B.....blond and beautiful! To which I would add, blond, beautiful and beyond! I didn't have to see her book. She didn't need a lens to make her beautiful. I can still remember her outfit. A casual blue silk suit that flowed with her every step. Before she even smiled or said a word, I detected something special in her. She walked right over to me, put out her hand, smiled and said,

"Hi, my name is Farrah Fawcett."

For a moment, I thought it was the start of another L.A. quake. I was rocked. I was in love! To quote Elvis, I was "all shook up!" Her smile was like no smile ever smiled at me. It hit me like a stun gun. Yes, the toothpaste Gods had smiled on me. They had sent me a toothpaste goddess. (Eat your hearts out, Crest and Colgate.)

She looked so fresh and young.....like she had just graduated college. She had! From the U. of Texas. This was her first job. Yes, it was I, dear friends, little ol' me who had found her and hired her! You'll never read it in *People* magazine or hear it on, *Entertainment Tonight*, but I'm happy just having you folks know it......I discovered Farah Fawcett! (Well, at least I got her started.)

On the day of the shoot, she arrived looking even more beautiful than I remembered. I told the director don't give her too much direction. Just let her go. I think she has just the right feeling and personality for this. And she sure knows how to use that smile. I was right. Her first take was perfect.....right out of the tube! It could have been a wrap. The director had nothing to add or change. Rarely have I seen a director with nothing to direct. Despite her perfection, I had her do about 12 more takes. I just wanted to watch her.

Folks, sitting out there watching Farrah do her thing.....toying with my words.....flirting with the lens.....blinding us with that smile.....I tell you, she was one hot Fawcett.

Shop Talk

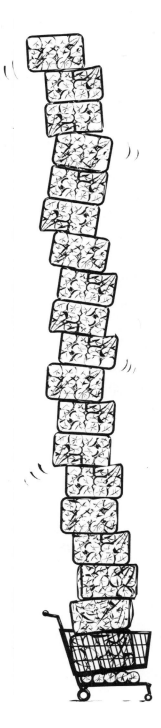

BRING A BIG CAR

We have become a pluralistic society. Let me define—we are a society where it has become exceedingly difficult to buy products in the quantity of one. You need an AAA or AA battery.....try to buy 1. You need 1 picture hook? Good luck. You need 1 straw or 1 egg or 1 shoe lace..... you're out of luck. You got a cold? You need a hankie? **A** hankie is hard to find. It's like finding 1 band aid or 1 paper clip. You need a pair of underwear? Try to buy 1 pair.

Nowhere is this lack of 1 more evident than in those mass market centers like Costco. You feel like you're shopping in a bare, down-to-the-bones warehouse. I call it "wherehouse" shopping because I never know where anything is. Here is a store that scorns 1 of anything. Here is bulk buying at its bulkiest best. Here is where people equip themselves for an atomic attack with enough detergent, batteries, shampoo, drinking water, antacids, snacks and dental floss to stay bunkered for months.

But Costco is at its bulk best when it comes to marketing the one necessity of life we can never afford to run out of....even for a day....or an hour! Indeed, nobody sells....nobody pushes....nobody moves toilet paper like Costco. (Move is a good word.) Toilet paper moves through Costco like.....well you know what. Try to buy 1 roll of the stuff. You have to buy it by the dozens. Every Costco features a monumental, skyscraper display of toilet paper that can only be described as, Mt. Charmin. (Mt. Brawny, too) I don't care how much toilet paper you got at home, you can't pass Mt. Charmin without grabbing another bundle. And Costco knows it! Even their carts are designed for toilet paper. You can slide your dozens right under the basket.

Indeed, toilet paper must be a big number in Costco's bottom line. ("Bottom line" is very apropos.) The competition is lagging far behind. ("Behind" is a great word.) They must be feeling great constipation—oops—I mean consternation. (This is a tough subject.)

I have an emotional tie to toilet paper. No, it has nothing to do with my infant, anal years. As an ad man, I once created an advertising campaign for a brand of toilet paper which shall remain nameless. Toilet paper is not an exciting writing assignment. It ranks down there with Sani Flush and Ty-D-Bol. My assignment was to find a creative, new way to talk about how soft and gentle this paper was. Never one to mince words, I came right to the point—

"It's Too Good For Toilet Paper!"

I can still remember the commercial—a guy in the bathroom yelling out to his wife, "Honey, where did you get this stuff? It's too good for toilet paper!" Beat that, Mr. Whipple! (That's for all you trivia-ites.)

With such a built-in, physiological demand for this product, it must be one of the great recession proof businesses. Or so I thought. Recently, I heard one of the big paper companies reported toilet paper sales down 8%. How can that be? Is Costco in trouble? I don't even want to know where the business went. That's a big loss but not a wipe out! (The perfect word!) I guess these toilet paper people are not as flush anymore. (Another perfect word!) Hey, I'm on a roll here. (Another great word!)

Enough of this talk. I'll let you go.

(I can't stop!)

WHAT'S YOUR RUSH?

Oh, the mind games we play when we have to get on a line—be it the supermarket, the movies, the bank, airport security or wherever. We always have to find the fastest line. We are consumed by speed.

You're at the supermarket and you have to get on a line. But you don't just get on any line. First you reconnoiter. You evaluate the load of groceries waiting in each line. Then you rate the checker. How fast does each one scan. And do they have a packer by their side or are they scanning <u>and</u> packing? Not good.

Most important, you check the shoppers. Avoid anybody holding coupons or a checkbook? Avoid mothers laden with strollers, toys and unruly tots. After carefully evaluating the situation, you end up with two finalists. Either get behind the guy in the brown shirt or get behind the lady in the blue dress. Just on a hunch, you go with "Brown Shirt."

Things are moving nicely. You keep checking your progress against "Blue Dress." You're ahead and pulling away. We got a horse race here....

It's "Brown Shirt" in the lead and pouring it on—"Blue Dress" is holding down second—

Then all of a sudden, your line hits a wall. The lady in front is arguing with the scanner about a 25 cent coupon. Neither side is giving in. The scanner calls for the manager. This could go to the Supreme Court.

"Brown Shirt" is falling back—"Blue Dress" is edging up—

If you were in your car, you would honk this lady off the road. But you have no horn.

It's "Brown Shirt" and "Blue Dress" now neck and neck—

Now comes the fatal error. You play the "If" game. If only I had ridden "Blue Dress." I would be in the lead. Self doubt starts creeping in. But you're stuck on "Brown Shirt."

It's "Blue Dress" pulling past "Brown Shirt" and opening a 1 cart lead—

They're still arguing about the coupon. The race is slipping away. You start thinking the unthinkable. Should I change lines?

"Blue Dress" looking strong—

Should I or shouldn't I?

Yes I should!

No I shouldn't!

It's "Blue Dress" and "Brown Shirt" still running one, two—

You start to go. You stop. You're torn apart. You're driving yourself crazy. Finally, you jump lines!

You're on "Blue Dress" the leader.

And here they come down the stretch—"Blue Dress" is wilting— the jock is giving her the whip but she's not responding—"Brown Shirt" is passing her—

Oh, God, "Brown Shirt" is nearing the finish line. Why did I do this? How stupid of me! I picked the winner. I guessed right. I threw it away. Should I go back to my old line? Will they take me back?" By now you need a couch and a psychiatrist.

My advice? Just stay home and get on line.

My wife can't take this kind of tension. She has a system. When we shop together, she'll get behind "Blue Dress" and I'll get behind "Brown Shirt." We split! Whoever hits pay dirt first, BAM!, the other runs over with their cart. I've gotten some mean glares from the back of the line. I have to be honest—I'm not proud of myself doing this. I feel like a cheater.

I have another confession to make. I've never told this to anyone—but I have gone through the Express line with more than 10 items.

Check this out—I've done 13!

Welcome, bookworms

"BOOK" THESE PEOPLE

I've noticed a new trend among some of my friends. They're penning their life stories. Yes, autobiographies! It's for the benefit of their children and grandchildren and hopefully even further generations. They want to leave them something more than just their IRA's. They want their family histories to live on. I think this is a noble deed, indeed.

Of course, biographies, whether auto or third person, have always been very popular reading. We love to peek into famous people's lives and get the dirt. So gather round all you biographers and historians. I've collected some fascinating subjects for you to bio. And to make it even easier, I have the titles ready to go.....so get out your pens.....

The life of terrorist king, Osama Bin Laden—
  "My Favorite Cave".

The married life of, Donald Trump—
  "One No Trump. Two No Trump."

The life of country music performer, Dolly Parton—
  "My Cup Runneth Over"

The private life of political powehouse, Nancy Pelosi—
  "I'm Speaker In My House, Too"

The life and works of, Michelangelo—
   "The Ceiling Needs A Painting"

The life and presidency of, Harry S. Truman—
   "DROP IT!"

The life of first lady, Hillary Clinton—
   "Sam, You Made The Pants Too Long"

The bellicose life of, Achmadinajad—
   "I Came! I Saw! I Ran!"

The life of eternally young, Joan Rivers—
   "About Face"

The glamorous life of, Elizabeth Taylor—
   "I Do. I Do. I Do. I Do. I Do. I Do."

The night life of, Dean Martin—
   "Pour Me"

The life of crazy man, Evel Knievel—
   "HOW DARE I!"

The life and genius of, Albert Einstein—
   "I Was Thinking"

The life of Yankee slugger, Roger Maris—
   "Asterisk"

The life and battles of, General Douglas MacArthur—
   "Many Happy Returns"

The life and works of, Sigmund Freud—
   "Pleasant Dreams"

YOU SAID IT!

Come all ye etymologists. Gather round. Today we will have a thoughtful, stimulating discussion of words.....or as you always say, "Let's talk etymology." Fear not. We will not discuss Latin derivations or secondary and tertiary meanings. Today I'd like to talk about simple words so you won't need your dictionaries or thesauruses. (Is that thesauri?)

English, like all languages, has some idiosyncratic twists and turns. There are certain phrases and expressions we use regularly without ever thinking about them. Where did they originate? Who coined them? And in some cases, when you look at them closely, what do they really mean? And I'm not talking about some arcane, erudite verbiage. I'm talking plain, everyday, good old English. (That's old, not olde.)

Take a common phrase like, "every now and then." Who decided it should be "every now and then" and not "every then and now." They mean the same. And who first called it, the "nitty-gritty" and not the "gritty-nitty?" Either way the nittty's gritty or the gritty's nitty. Same for these standards—"the long and short of it"—"out and about"—"this and that—"back and forth." Try them in reverse. They all work.

Another common phrase—"It was a hotly contested debate with a lot of of give and take." Why isn't that "take and give?" Many times I've taken it and then given it. I like that better, because I want to end up on the giving end. It's that last licks mentality.

Now here's a thought you've spoken many times and never given it a second thought. (Not even a first thought.)

"Everyone was talking at once so I couldn't get a word in edgewise."

My advice? Use thinner words. But let's pursue this fitting problem a bit further. If you say, "I can't get a word in edgewise," do you then say, "I can't get a thought in lengthwise?"

Let's keep going. "That cold drink really hit the spot." What spot? Where is this ubiquitous spot? Is it above or below the waistline? Who first found it? Has it ever been seen on an MRI? Is this spot operable? Have you ever spotted this spot?

And how do we describe that moment when one's words are a total embarrassment, a monumental faux pas? We say he "stuck his foot in his mouth." More than blundering talk, "One's foot in their mouth," speaks of an incredible physical feat. If you ever saw it done, it would probably leave you "tongue tied".....which is physically even more spectacular than the foot feat.

We have some quirky expressions in sports lingo, too. "He pitched a great game. He really cut the mustard." I've poured, squeezed, squirted and shmeared mustard. If somebody would show me how to cut it, I'd cut it with relish.

It's flu season and you've got a cold and cough. As they say, you're "under the weather." Aren't we always under the weather? Isn't the weather always above us? Come to think of it, the weather is also all around us. So when you're ailing you might say, "I'm amid the weather." How about when you're flying and you've got a cold. You could say you're under the weather.....over the weather. That's English for 'ya!

Here's one you hear on the news. "The robbers broke into the store in broad daylight." Is broad daylight followed by narrow daylight?

And then there's the classic....."He was cursing out the speaker under his breath." This guy must have been a ventriloquist. It makes you wonder.....if you're mad and you're shouting insults, are you shouting "<u>over</u> your breath?"

And finally, in these anxious economic times, it's nice to know our language holds the line on inflation. Imagine if it didn't—

"The brakes on my car are great. They stop on a quarter."

"You have a distant look. A nickel for your thoughts."

That's probably a dime now.

My Mrs. never misses.

I CANCELED MY INTERNET. MY WIFE KNOWS EVERYTHING

Looking back, I had so many, many good teachers throughout my schooling. I can remember, Mrs. Powers, who drummed dreaded English grammar into my head so I'd never forget it. I'm still using it today. Then there was Mr. Van Vleck in high school, who opened my eyes to the incredible story of America's founding. And, in college, I was fortunate to take Professor Van Nostrand's course on American literature. Made me want to write.

But of all my teachers there is one who has taught me more about real, every day life than any other. This is a teacher who has taught me practical, usable, everyday smarts. This is my wife.....my beloved Professor! Does any of the following sound familiar, guys?

I go to the supermarket with my Professor. We're walking down the dairy aisle. As she reaches for some butter, she says, "Honey, grab a milk."

Now I know in advance, if I grab a milk from the front row, she'll say, "No, honey—take from the back row. That's where they put the freshest milk. They keep the oldest milk in front—so they'll sell that first." Just like the milk, the lesson is Grade A.

In response, I'm dying to say, "Honey, do you think these people got to be the success they are by accident? They have over 100 supermarkets. Do you think they're stupid? They know what you women are doing.

They put the oldest milk in the back row and the freshest in the front." That's what I'd like to say but I can't offend my teacher, my beloved Professor. So I dutifully take a milk from the back row and move on to the cottage cheese. Where I also take from the back row.

Here's another lesson well learned. When we go out to dine, my wife has taught me, "You never take the first table." Why? Because it's right under an air conditioning duct.....or it's too close to the kitchen.....or it's stuck away in a dark corner.....or the little tot at the next table could wake up any minute, cranky and hungry. Make the hostess work. Go table shopping.

And while we're on the subject of dining, here's a problem that's always embarrassed me. I always ate off the wrong bread plate and drank the other guy's water. Then my wife taught me one of the "10 Commandments" of dining etiquette. (She's a regular Mrs. Moses.)

Thou shalt eat from thy left and drink from thy right

I never knew that. I never learned it in school. My mother never taught it to me.....but my wife did and I've never forgotten it. Now I hate it when some boor crumbs up my bread plate with his roll or some Neanderthal grabs my water. Don't these guys have wives?

But the greatest lesson my wife has taught me is how to check into a hotel.....especially those European hotels where they always try to stick Americans with the worst rooms. I've learned the routine.

A suave gentleman comes to show us to our room. I tell the bellman to leave the luggage. I take a seat and wait in the lobby. My wife goes up with Mr. Suave to check out the room. Within 3 minutes, Mr. Suave will come hustling down to get more keys and then race back upstairs to my waiting wife. Finally he invites me to follow him to the room my wife has selected. At this point, a little of the suave has worn off Mr. S.

Yes, it's true folks—I would have picked the wrong milk, the wrong cottage cheese and eaten off your bread plate. Even worse, I would have taken the first table and first hotel room. But give me credit—
I picked the right wife.

P
R
N
D

I went to college with a guy who became a very successful playwright. He had a Broadway hit which was made into a movie and won an Oscar. I think it even won a Pulitzer. The name of the play was, "*Driving Miss Daisy*." I have a very similar idea for a play—"*Driving Mrs. Bushell*." The dialogue writes itself.

"You're driving too close to the yellow line."

"Why didn't you turn left there?"

"Get away from this truck."

"You're too close to the car in front of you."

"Why are you driving so slowly?"

"Why are you driving so fast?"

"Stop driving so herky jerky. I'm trying to put on my makeup."

Yes, my wife is anything but a quiet, passive passenger. I may be driving the car but she is driving me. I am merely an instrument of her will. My wife must always take the shortest, quickest route. She is obsessed with shortcuts. (Maybe that's because she's always late.) I think she has a shortcut gene geneticists have yet to discover.

She is so determined to find the shortest way, she actually tests one route against the other. She times them and clocks their mileage. She counts the number of lights along each route. I didn't know it at the time, but I married a map. With all due apologies to you mathematicians, allow me to correct one of geometry's most famous theorems.....the shortest distance between two points is.....my wife.

An example: I'm coming up to my left turn. It's a red arrow. Straight ahead is green. As I start to move into the left turn lane, my wife pokes me....."No, go straight through the green. Up there make a U-turn. Come back and make the right on red." I obey. As I make the right on red, she pokes me again and points....."See, you'd still be over there behind the Chevy waiting to turn left." Unsaid....."Aren't you glad you have me." Total time saved.....8.5 seconds.

The real problem I have is when I turn on my car's navigation system. Now I have 2 ladies telling me where to go. Now my wife has competition. Another female is entering her domain of expertise threatening to debunk all her research on shortcuts. The two get along like my wife would get along with my mistress.....if I had a mistress. The navigation lady opens her big mouth......

"Prepare to make a right turn 100 yards ahead."

"Don't listen to her. I know a short cut. Keep going straight."

"Prepare to turn right 50 feet ahead."

"Don't turn. That's the long way."

"You missed the turn. Proceed to the intersection ahead and turn to go back."

"Go back? Never!"

"50 yards ahead turn left at the intersection and proceed back."

"Who are you going to listen to.....some lady in your dashboard or your wife? Your girlfriend should get a map."

"Honey, look! She is a map!"

Now, I'd like to see by a show of hands, how many of you think I turned around and went back? And how many think I went straight ahead? Well, I was saved by the Traffic Gods. When I got to the U-turn, there was a big sign.....**"No U-turns Allowed."** Whew!

I think my wife missed her calling. Had she lived back in the 1800's, when settlers were pushing America ever westward.....when adventurous men were charting and mapping new routes and passages to the Pacific.....had she lived back then, today we would be celebrating the exploits of Lewis & Clark & Bushell.

Excuse me, dear.....Bushell & Lewis & Clark.

If it wasn't for my doctors,

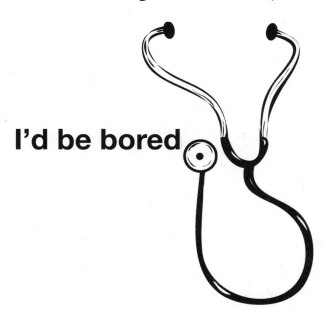

I'd be bored

WHERE DOES IT HURT?

For me, a great morning is any morning I wake up. I think the secret to long life is to keep waking up. The next good thing is to get out of bed and take a few healthy strides. One recent morning, I took one stride and stopped short. I felt a new pain in a new place. What's this? I've never hurt there. What could be wrong there? I'm in trouble. I don't have a doctor for there. Even worse, I don't have insurance for there!

I called a buddy who has more pains in more places than any man I know. He came up with the perfect doctor for my new pain in a new place. "Go see, Doctor Heal. He's a genius." I lost no time.

"Hello. you've reached the office of Dr. Heal."

"Hi, I'd like to make an appointment."

"Do you have insurance?"

"Don't you want to know what's wrong with me first?"

"After your insurance." I gave her my insurance.

"What do you want to see Dr. Heal about?"

"I woke up this morning with a new pain in a new place."

"I can give you tomorrow at 1:30 p.m.. Make sure you bring both insurance cards, your driver's license, a credit card and your birth certificate."

Next afternoon, I headed for my new doctor for my new pain in a new place. I looked for his name in the lobby directory and found him listed with 9 other doctors. I'm not seeing Dr. Heal. I'm seeing Dr.

Heal, Inc.. Ten doctors! I was worried about the wait time. My fears were well founded. When I walked into his waiting room, I thought I was at the Motor Vehicle Bureau. There must have been 40 people waiting.

Me and my new pain in a new place could be there for days. I took one of the few remaining seats and started to analyze the situation.

10 doctors for 40 patients is not so bad. Maybe 3 or 4 patients a doctor. I was feeling better.

Not so fast, Gordon. What makes you think all 10 doctors are working today. Probably not. That's why there are 10 of them. So they don't have to work every day. Or nearly every day.

Let's suppose 5 doctors are here. That's like 8 patients a doctor. I'm getting depressed. But wait a minute.....it could be even worse.

I'm assuming every doctor has the same number of patients. I can't assume that assumption. One may have a bigger practice.....ergo more patients. The 40 waiters could break 12-8-7-7-6. And with my luck, my guy's got 12.

And then it hit me.....the worst case scenario. How many of Dr. Heal's patients have the same 1:30 appointment I have? Am I the last of the 1:30's to arrive? I had to know. I stood up.

"Excuse the interruption ladies and gentlemen. But would all the people who have a 1:30 appointment with Dr. Heal please raise their hands." Before a hand could be raised, the nurse sprang to her feet.

"Mr. Bushell, that is privileged information. Please sit down with your new pain in a new place. Your turn will come."

They don't want you to know.

GIMME SOME SKIN

I'm almost afraid to say this, but for a long time now, I have thought we are being invaded by extra terrestrials.....ETs! Beings from outer space are infiltrating our society pretending to be one of us. Steven Spielberg had it right. He knew. He's a regular Nostradamus, that Steven!

I never mentioned my fears before because I didn't want to start another national panic like the one that followed Orson Welles' infamous, "Invasion of Mars" radio show. But have you noticed how many people are walking around amongst us wearing band aids and bandages. They wear them on their nose.....on their chin.....on their forehead.....on their ear lobe.....all over their arms and legs. And these ET's are everywhere. The malls. The movies. The restaurants. Are these bandages a sign? Is this how they identify each other?

And then I realized how foolish of me. No need to fear. These bandaged brigades aren't coming from Mars.....they're coming from the dermatologist.....or as I like to call call him, "The Snipper." Because that's how it always starts. "I'm just going to take a snip of this red spot here."

I think the "Snippers" have a motto.....a credo by which they practice....."A Snip A Trip!" Let me ask you this.....have you ever left the dermatologist's office un-snipped? You always leave a snip or two of you behind. My "Snipper" never misses a spot. Nothing escapes him. Last week, he took a snip from a spot on me that has never seen the sun. I mean, the sun has never shone where my "snipper" snipped.

Yes, folks, the villain in this matter is old Mr. Sun. We used to worship him. We would bathe in his rays, all greased up, basking in his warmth.

With reflectors, no less!

We "microwaved" ourselves.

We were beautiful people.....tan 'n golden.....grilled to perfection. How we loved, Sunny. He's a big reason why we bought in Florida. They even named the state after him....."The Sunshine State." Now they should change all the license plates to, "The Sunbloc State."

Today you don't step outside wtihout sunbloc. And we can't gop on enough of the stuff. So we walk around with a pasty white complexion and we sweat a cream color. Palefaces! We look like we haven't been outside for weeks. You see people walking around with left over bloc in their eyebrows. Check out their ear lobes. More bloc. Strangest of all, peolpe go to the beach and cover themselves in bloc. Then they sit in the sun. No comprendo.

Yes, the "Snipper" is big on bloc. He's also fanatical about getting out all the bad stuff. In this area, The "Snipper" does not work alone. Oh no, this is too big a job for one man. When the lab report indicates the "Snipper" must snip deeper, he has an accomplice.....an expert. Enter the "Slicer." Who knows how deep to go? The Mohs knows! The Mohs is an artiste. He slices and slices real thin until you're clean.

The "Snipper" and the "Slicer".....this is starting to sound like Deli talk. Except we're the corned beef.

THE JOINTS AIN'T JUMPIN'

Some day, I'm going to write a book. A serious book. A quasi-medical book. I already have the title: *"I Married A Bad Back."* Then my wife can write the book she has always wanted to write: *"I Married A Bad Hip."* She already knows what her second book will be: *"I Married A Bad Hip And A Worse Shoulder."* We make some pair. Probably a lot like many of you pairs out there. Maybe knees, necks or ankles are your thing.

Thank, God, we have the best joint doctors down here in Florida. I guess they're good because they get lots of practice. If any young med school students are reading this, I strongly urge you to become an osteo-anything. You will get them streaming into your office by the thousands, hunched and limping, canes and all. You will be loved and revered. If one day you decide to retire, I guarantee, there will be a "cane" mutiny.

As with any medical specialty, there are doctors and then there is, "The One" in that field....The God! Yes, there is a Knee God. A Hip God. A Shoulder God." This is the doctor you must find. How do you find him? Don't listen to your cousin who works with a lady who has an uncle who.....forget all that. Go right to the patients. Go to the people who have had the operation you need. Who knows better? Where do you find these patients?

Go to any pool. They're walking, flexing, bending, stretching, rotating, dunking. Recovering! Ask them how they're doing. Did their doctor do a good job? If they think he's a God, get his name. But before you operate, get some new bathing suits. You wanna look good.

You also have to find the best hospital for your joint. There is one hospital deemed the numero uno place for knees. Same for hips, Same for shoulders. The problem is your knee God may not operate in the numero uno knee hospital. Sorry, you can't always have the best of both.

Who says you can't? We have to build a new hospital. A hospital dedicated to joint sufferers. State of the art. No steps. No ramps. Only moving sidewalks, escalators and elevators. And the hip God, the knee God and the shoulder God, with their disciples, will come to perform their miracles here. It will be a Lourdes for our limbs. And all the joint sufferers will get down on their knees to say, "Thank you." (Maybe not the knee sufferers.)

And we shall call this new healing edifice, this new monument to our moving parts:

THE JOINT

And now for a commercial.

Don't touch that bipper!

SWEDE TALK

Have you ever been to the Smithsonian in Washington? It's a prestigious, imposing collection of American history. What I'm about to say, I say with great pride and a heavy dose of humility. Yours truly is in the Smithsonian. No, there's no bust of me on a pedestal. I suspect I'm in the archives with a few million other memorabilia. But in.....is <u>in</u>!

So what got me in? I came in via Madison Avenue. Seems I wrote a TV commercial that gained the kind of fame the Smithsonian considers a landmark worthy of inclusion in its collection of American Advertising. In its time, the commercial really burst upon the scene. It used a selling tool hitherto considered taboo for prime time TV. It used sex.

Go back to the 60's. America was a prim and proper place. Victorian ruled. There was no such thing as cable TV so there was nothing to watch but good, wholesome network programming. This was the moral mood of the country when I got to work on a new client..... Noxzema Shave Cream.

The sales problem? With a name like Noxzema, men thought of it as a medicated shave cream. You had to have a skin problem to use it. The challenge? How do we make Noxzema a shave cream for swingers who want to look sexy and get plenty of girls. How do we talk "sex" in a very prim and proper society?

I knew I had to promise a close shave but how can I talk about it in a new, sexy way. The word "naked" popped into my head. "Noxzema leaves your face naked." Now that's a close shave! That's sexy!

Thinking "naked" led me to "strippers." And "strippers" led me to the eternal cry from the balcony....."Take it off.....Take it all off!" This is about men taking it off.....stripping (shaving). Wow! That sounds hot. But I needed some executional punch. I got it with music. A guy will shave to the same music strippers strip to.....David Rose's famous, bump n' grind, "Stripper." As I remembered it, the music was the perfect beat to shave to. I ran out and got a copy. I put it on, grabbed a razor and started shaving to the music. It was perfect.

Now, who would tell the men to "Take it off?" I found a beautiful, Swedish lady named, Gunila Knudson, who purred "Take it off" with a sexy Swedish accent, which made it even sexier. A gorgeous Swedish blond can turn any American male into an animal. (A Tiger?) She became almost as famous as the commercial.

So let's put all the pieces together. I had a good looking, young guy "stripping" to hot "Stripper" music while a ravishing Swedish blond urged him to, "Take it off.....Take it all off!" I'll tell you what I had. I had dy-na-mite!

The spot went on the air and the reaction was immediate. It was the talk of Mad. Ave. and Main St......and the women of America, too. Almost immediately, the client started getting nasty letters from irate women who thought the spot was filthy and disgusting. The women were up in arms. They threatened to boycott all Noxzema products unless Noxzema "took it off" the air. The threats of boycott grew so loud, the spot was pulled from the air after only a few weeks.

I was heart broken. My claim to fame was no more. But the men of America saved the day. When the sales results for that period came in, the shave cream numbers were up so dramatically, the client decided to put the "Stripper" back on the air.

Does advertising work? In its first year, the "Stripper" commercial doubled Noxzema shave cream sales. Doubled! I hate to think how close I came to losing my best commercial ever. How close Noxzema came to losing a sales bonanza. How close the Smithsonian came to losing an American classic. And how close American men came to losing sight of Gunila.

It was a close shave.

FIRST PRIZE: $50 MILLION

Today, I have a parable for you.....a tale with an important lesson. The lesson is Solomonic in its wisdom, so learn it well.

Back in the 70's, when I was a hard working advertising man, Datsun cars, now called Nissan, decided to move their mega account from their Los Angeles ad agency to a New York shop. Up to that point, it was the largest account to ever change agencies in the history of the advertising business.....50 million bucks big! Back then, that was monster big! It was all the advertising world could talk about, Who will get Datsun? Who will have the BIG IDEA?

As I recall, Datsun started by talking to 15 qualified N.Y. agencies, including mine, William Esty Company. The pundits gave us no chance. We were a package goods agency. What did we know about cars? The favorite was Wells, Rich, Green.....a hot creative shop.

In a series of pressure packed meetings, the list was cut from 15 agencies to 5 and then to 3 finalists. The pundits be damned.....we were in the final 3.

Through all those meetings, nobody had yet presented any work on Datsun. That was saved for the big finale. The client would return to New York in 3 weeks to hear an all day presentation from each of the 3 finalists on how they would advertise Datsun. It was "put up or shut up" time. We picked straws to see who would go first. I picked the lead off spot. I was delighted. By the time they get to the third agency, they will be sated, exhausted, bored and homesick.

Then came the real show biz touch. How would the winning agency know they won? Well, the client would fly back to L.A.....meet amongst themselves and pick a winner. Once decided, they would call the winner and invite them to lunch at New York's trendy, "21 Club."

So who got invited to lunch? Who had the "Big Idea"? You know I wouldn't build this up and then tell you somebody else won. The winning $50 million idea was **"Datsun.....We Are Driven."** (Biggest idea I ever had!) We not only won the 50 million, we got a fancy, free lunch. Now you probably want to know the important Solomonic lesson I promised. I'll leave that to my son, Alan.....

"I was 16 at the time, folks, and a real car nut. If Dad wins this account, I'll learn to drive in a Datsun Z car. Awesome! I was in school when I called home and got the awesome news. After school, I went to caddy at a local golf course. I was carrying bags for two men when I overheard one say, "Did you hear who won the Datsun account?" The other answered, "No, but I'm sure it was Wells, Rich."

I piped right in, "Wells, Rich didn't win." They whirled around and looked at this young kid in torn jeans and an old sweat shirt. How could he possibly know the big news on Mad. Ave..

"How do you know?"

"Trust me, I know." I didn't want to tell them how I knew. I was afraid they wouldn't tip me as well if they knew who my father was. Then they asked me, "Who won it?" I proudly told them, "William Esty." Like everyone else, they were shocked

When I told my father the story that night, he said, 'Learn a lesson from that, Alan. Watch where you talk. You never know who's listening.' Awesome lesson, Dad."

Alan banged up the Z car twice in the first 6 months.
Awesome!

Do you get teed off, too?

GOLF IS A TEST
(TAKE IT)

As a rule, golfers are not a happy crowd. Rarely do you hear them raving about their game. Just look at the handicaps. The 14-16's are now 18-20. The 17-19's are now 23-25. The 26-28's are now playing cards.

What's behind this trend? Certainly not the equipment. I'm sure you play with the highest tech, most perfectly balanced, titanium clubs made. I'm sure you tee off with the longest distance golf balls made. And I'm sure you spend endless hours on the driving range practicing what the pro taught you in your weekly lesson. All this dedication and devotion, and still you're not happy with your game. (And I'm being kind.)

That's because golf is not played with clubs. You play golf with your head. It's not your metals.....it's your mettle. Can your psyche handle the up and down emotions.....the frustrations.....the disappointments of golf? You don't need Titanium clubs. You need a Titanium psyche. Here's a little psyche-logical test. See if your psyche is psyched for golf.

- Do you feel sorry for the person who gets you as a partner?
- Have you ever 4 putted from 12 feet.....and needed a "gimme" for #4?
- Do you start thinking about lunch on the front nine?
- On average, how many bugs a round do you kill?

\ When you enter your score on the computer, do you require privacy?

\ Have you played 18 holes worth of golf after only 9?

\ When you're on the first tee with 3 other strangers and they ask for handicaps.....do you whisper?

\ Are you bad on the course but good on the range? Or are you never good?

\ Are you always "away."

\ Could you give up golf if you had something better to do? Any thing to do?

\ When they make up bets on the first tee, do you think, "That's good. I can only lose $10."

\ Is your idea of positive thinking, "I'm positively terrible."

\ Are you tired of hearing you have great potential?

\ Do you ever get two good rounds in a row? Two good holes in a row? Two good shots in a row?

\ When you chip, do you end up further from the hole then when you started?

\ Do you pray for rain a lot?

\ When you throw a club in anger.....does it slice?

\ Do you take out your frustrations on the golf cart?

\ After you hit your first tee shot, how fast do you reach for the mulligan in your pocket—.05 sec.—.03 sec.—.01 sec.?

\ When there's a lake between you and the green, do you imagine your ball on the green or in the lake?

\ Which goes further.....your ball or the divot?

\ Do you live in constant fear of hitting that dread shot that starts with "Sh?" Are your fears founded?

\ What's your favorite excuse for your bad play? I've got a bad back. I haven't played in weeks. I'm on this pill.

\ What's your favorite putter? Your partner?

\ Are you sorry you ever read this?

FORE-GET IT!

Golf is a wonderful teacher. A trip around the course is a lesson in self control, concentration and yes, sportsmanship. I've learned the sportsmanship bit but I'm afraid I still haven't gotten a diploma in the other classes.

However, I've learned another important lesson playing golf.....I shouldn't be playing it. It goes even deeper than that. I shouldn't play any sport where you have to hit a ball. It's a very sobering lesson because it eliminates so many other games I could be out there enjoying.

Tennis anyone? Not I, thanks. Yes, the tennis racket is bigger than a golf club and the ball is bigger, too. Should be easier. But a tennis ball is speeding at you.....moving and spinning. How can I expect to hit such a moving missile when I can't hit a little white ball that's just sitting there, perfectly still, on a lush tuft of grass, just waiting to be whacked.

And there are other ball-hitting games. Baseball? Same moving ball problem. Polo? Tough to find a game. Cricket? Even tougher to find a game. Badminton? There are no games. Volleyball? The sand gets into everything.

So I'm stuck with golf. The trouble with me and golf is five fold:

Fold 1: I have no "feel" for golf. Some days I go to the driving range to warm up. I pick up a club and right away my hands say, "What's this? Are we playing a new game. This thing feels strange." Do you feel for me, folks?

Golf also takes "touch". Putting is where "touch" really counts. I'm totally out of "touch". I'll tell you how out of "touch" I am. I once had to yell, "Fore" on the putting green.

Fold 2: I have no consistency. Sure, very golfer has good and bad days. Some days their game is on. Some days it's off. My game is on a dimmer. It's up, it's down.....from day to day, hole to hole, swing to swing.

Fold 3: Good golfers have good muscle memory. I have no memory for anything. I can't even remember my starting times. And when I finally get on the green, and they ask me how many I lie, I can't remember the beginning of the hole.

I handle my lack of muscle memory with a special pre-shot routine. Before I swing, I lean over and whisper right into my left shoulder. "Lefty, you have to start the swing. You have to turn around me. Don't do your swing and sway thing." Three seconds later I swing.....you guessed it.....Lefty forgot!

Fold 4: You have to have rhythm to play golf. I don't care if or you once played drums or you can tap dance to "Tea For Two." None of this means you have the golf beat. Golf demands grace, ease and smoothness.

Golf instructors always say if you can count to three, you can hit the ball. As you make your back swing, just count slowly to yourself.....one.....two.....three.....hit. I've used that system. I even count out loud to make sure I hear myself. I count one..... ***twothreehit!***

Fold 5: Putting everything else aside, the #1 asset you can have in golf is good eye-hand coordination. I can report I have good eye-hand coordination in one aspect of the game.

Driving the cart.

I miss you Walter Cronkite.

WE INTERRUPT
THIS BOOK...

I find it hard to watch the news these days. Bad news is not good news and there seems to be nothing but bad news. Is there no place left on earth where nice, happy things are happening?

This bad news glut is even more apparent with the advent of cable. Network television gives you bad news only every few hours. But cable sates you with 24/7, non-stop, round-the-clock bad news. They may change programs and reporters, but they repeat the same depressing stories, interviews and footage over and over again. Change channels and they're reporting the same bad news. Is there no escape from this litany of bad?

Yes, there is! And it can happen at any time. Suddenly they will cut away from the anchor. Exciting, pulsating, music blares out. "BREAKING NEWS" flashes across the screen. You're awakened from your bad news stupor. You might even sit up! What's this all about? Gather round all. Wake up out there—we have NEW bad news. JUST IN! Here's bad news you haven't heard yet. BRAND NEW bad news! It might be new riots—new floods—new hostages—new Dow Jones tremors!

You can feel the energy level rise in the news room. The anchor's pace quickens. He speaks with new drama and urgency. He's up! He's just been handed NEW bad news. He needed NEW bad news as much as we did.

Maybe the NEW bad news is a killer hurricane headed for our coast. Reporters are on the beaches, on the docks, at the hospitals, at the beach front hotels. They're poised with their grim faces and dire voices, ready to bring you all the NEW bad news live from inside the hurricane. This is NEW bad news reporting at its best!

And then the hurricane suddenly swerves away from us. There's nothing to report. No flooding. No damage. No loss of life. The director doesn't know what to do. The sun is out!

Cable does something else that makes it hard to watch the news. They give you two different news stories at once. While the anchor reports on the latest from Afghanistan, a tape runs across the bottom of the screen reporting the latest on the Tiger affair. Afghanistan or Tiger? Should I listen or should I read? I've tried doing both at the same time but I'm not compartmentalized enough.

Even more distracting than this, the cable news shows have added the most distracting distraction of all.....women.....gorgeous women. Yes, all cable news shows now have an anchor and an anchorette. (Weatherettes, financialettes and sportsettes, too.) Have you noticed..... the anchorettes all look the same.....beautiful with long, flowing, perfectly coiffed blond hair. And they talk beautifully and sound like they all come from the same state.....the same city.....the same block. Do they clone all these "blond & beautifuls" on a news farm somewhere?

And these "blond & beautifuls" are all built to do the news, too..... trim and shapely. They may be giving you bad news but they are good news to the eye. Needless to say, the cable producers take full advantage of this plus. The ladies are not always seated behind the traditional news desk. Often they do the news in full view.....seated on a high chair..... legs fully extended to the floor. And I mean legs. These gals got some gams. It should come as no news, they like to wear their skirts above the knees so you can't miss the gams. (But can miss the news.)

Between the anchor talking, the tape moving across the screen and these shapely, leggy, lovelies talking to me, I don't know what to watch. Maybe it's just me, but despite all this high tech and glamour, I miss you, Walter Cronkite.

READ MY DRIVEWAY

I believe in staying up to the second with world news. We are living in such a news busy world, where major events that effect our lives, are happening every day. I want to know what is happening in the Far East, the Mid East, Europe, Africa, South America.

As a result, I subscribe to 4 newspapers. In the morning my driveway looks like the President's desk. (Maybe not Bush's.) Of course I get *The New York Times*. You have to be able to say you get *The New York Times*. Even better, you want people to see the *Times* in your driveway. It says you are well read and worldly wise. Early morning joggers are very impressed.

I also get the *Wall Street Journal*. I don't play the market. I don't even understand selling long and short. But the *Wall Street Journal* is another paper you want people to see in your driveway. It has a cachet. People think you're rich and smart, (I'm neither).

I wouldn't be without our local paper. It could report the most important news of all. It tells me what's playing, where it's playing and what time it's playing.

There amongst my newspapers, you'll also see the latest edition of the *Palm Beach Shiny Sheet*. Living in South Florida as I do, this is a must. This is the paper that takes you inside Palm Beach high society. It doesn't get higher than that. The paper reeks of Worth Ave. and polo players and is populated with very elegant, rich society people. They're so upscale they're off the scale. I feel funny reading about such fancy folk in my pajamas. I should get dressed for this paper.

If you jogged by my house early one morning, you would be very impressed with my reading material.....not only the quantity but the quality. Every morning I get up, put on a robe and go outside to fetch my papers. I bring them into the kitchen, unwrap them and brew up a quick cup of coffee. Now I'm ready for the news. So I turn on *CNN* or *Fox* and get it spoon-fed to me. Let's face it, folks, it's easier to watch it than read it.

My newspapers sit there undisturbed. And that's where they sit until I get home from dinner. I bring them into the bedroom for a quick scan before bedtime. But alas, not even the *New York Times* with it's editorial brilliance or the *Wall Street Journal* with its economic insights, can compete with *American Idol* or 24 or *Dancing With The Stars*.

I just hope none of my neighbors or the joggers by my house read this. It would be real news to them.

**They say today's retirees
lead a full life.**

**Eat out 7 nights a week,
and you would, too.**

GIVING ORDERS

Read any good menus lately? I have a lot of trouble reading them these days. Maybe it's just me but the type is getting smaller and smaller. Do they think tiny type is more elegant? I have done a survey of restaurant menus and I have found that the smaller the type, the more bloated the price and the scantier the portions. So if you get a menu that nobody at the table can read, better have some rolls and a hefty appetizer because the main course alone is going to leave you famished.

I even have trouble reading the entrees.....the biggest words on the menu. And forget about the "come withs." Trying to make out the potatoes and vegetables, is like trying to read the bottom line on an eye chart. Wait a minute! I just hit on a great idea for all you ophthalmologists. Why listen to your patients recite that boring, B—S—L—Q—R— all day. Forget the eye charts. Hand them a menu.

"Now, Mrs. Brown, hold the patch over your right eye and tell me what comes with the Chicken Bolinka." Now you're cookin', Doc!

But the problem is not merely the type. I think many of today's restaurant architects graduated from the minimalist school of lighting. They've been taught, "Go light on the light." Keep it dim. Shadowy. Sexy. This is what makes a restaurant chic and sophisticated. Their idea is a few 20 watt bulbs behind yellow lenses giving little splashes of light here and there. If you're not getting splashed, forget about reading what's for dinner. I don't like my light in splashes. I wanna be drowned in it!

Another favorite minimalist lighting trick is a little, flickering candle on every table That little romantic flicker really lights up the ladies.....but not the menu! Even worse, I can't see my food. "Honey, pass the candle. I can't see what this brown stuff on my plate is."

"I'll take the candle after you, Gordon."

I admit not everyone has my menu problems. I have a friend who enjoys reading food as much as eating it. He reads a menu like he's reading Tolstoy. He's smart. He comes to dine with a teeny, weeny flashlight He reads and savors every word on the menu. Sometimes I ask him to read a dish for me. That's only if somebody else is using the candle.

Aside from bad food, I think the worst thing a restaurant can be known for is bad service. People do not like long waits between courses. I was having lunch with a friend who likes to have his food before he even orders it. He likes to eat and be gone! We were waiting for our food and it didn't look like "gone" was coming soon. He called over the captain.

"Captain, we just ordered two sandwiches. What could take so long?"

"I'm sorry, sir. I'll get on it. Do you remember what your waitress looked like?"

"Yes. She was blond, petite and very cute. But I don't know what she looks like now."

WEIGHT TIL YOU READ THIS!

Today we have a special guest.....a renowned expert on weight loss. His unorthodox, revolutionary research in the field of diet and human weight control is causing quite a stir in the medical world. Meet, Dr. Thinny .

Dr. Thinny, I know you already have an army of loyal and devoted fat followers who swear by your system. We're ready to enlist. What do we have to do?

"Thank you, Gordon. I have found a major cause of weight gain which has been totally ignored by doctors and scientists. Based on this finding, I have designed a program that's guaranteed to take off pounds. It's not a diet. It doesn't deal with consumption levels. I have formulated a regimen.....a very hard regimen to follow. It demands total dedication and incredible will power. You can't cheat. You must resist all temptation."

"Well, what do I have to do?"

"Forget about carbs and cookies and calorie counting. This does not involve injections or pills. You and your partner must start a new way of life today. You can't put it off. You must make a pledge now. You must take an oath that from this day forward, every day of the week, you will.....EAT HOME!

No matter how many fabulous new restaurants open.....no matter how many friends invite you out to dinner, you must tell them you can't go because you're eating home. Even if they fall over from shock, even if the phone line goes dead at the other end, you will eat home. This is going to be very difficult for you to do because you must first overcome a major stumbling block.

"What's the stumbling block?"

Before you can eat home.....you must first find your kitchen. It should be a nice size room with a sink, a refrigerator, an oven and a dishwasher. It should be right near your dining room.....if you know where that is. Once found, get acquainted with your kitchen. Find out how everything works. A note of caution. Before you try the oven, first open it and take out the pamphlets and papers inside. These are your instructions and 2-year warrantee, which probably lapsed a long time ago. You may also want to dust off your oven. Do the same with your dishwasher. As a matter of fact, dust the whole kitchen.

Now this is very important.....make sure you find your microwave oven. This is critical. For you, "cook" is a 4 letter word. You're not going to peal, cut, slice, dice, stew, heat, bake, boil or broil. Maybe, if you're not too tired, you'll rinse a little. This is why your microwave is your best friend. You'll use it more than anything else because you'll probably bring in all your meals already cooked and prepared. You'll just have to warm them up in the microwave. And let me tell you, after all these years of eating out, there's nothing like sitting down to a good, home, warmed up meal.

"Well, Doc, I have great news. Yesterday my wife and I decided to try your system. We resisted all temptation and we ate home.

"That's great, Gordon."

"Let me tell you, Doc, she made one helluva breakfast!"

How do geese know when to flock south?

They flock when we flock.

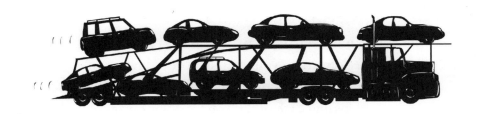

WHO'S
WHATS-HIS-FACE?

One of my favorite times down here in Florida is our annual Homecoming. No, I'm not talking about football games or Homecoming queens waving from the back of open convertibles. I'm talking about our kind of Homecoming.....that wonderful time every Fall, when the Snowflake folks leave their northern abodes, make like geese and fly back south for the winter. It's a time for excited hello's, warm hand shakes and hearty hugs. And everybody is asking, "How have you been?" and "How was your summer?"

And of course, you know what else comes with Homecoming. Before you even come down, call the plumber, the roofer, the electrician, the cable guy. Set up appointments in advance. You know what awaits you as soon as you walk through your front door.

Somewhere the roof will be leaking. Somewhere a toilet will be running. Somewhere switches won't work. And for sure, even though it's 80 degrees out, it will be snowing on all your TV's. Homecoming is expensive. But true to Murphy's Law, none of this ever happens when you're there all winter. Only when you go away.

But this is not the hardest part of homecoming. Even worse than these home breakdowns, is your memory breakdown. You've been away for just a few months but it might as well have been years. Everybody is hugging and kissing each other. You're walking around nodding and waving to everyone and you have no idea of anyone's name, And they have no idea of yours.

It's time to get creative! It's game time! Time to play, "Fake That Name." Ah, the art of the name fake. Women excel at it. For example: "Well, look who's back in town.....our bridge captain. You look great, darling." Did I miss the ladies' name? Is she, "Mrs. Bridge Captain?"

Men pull off the "Name Fake" in a blink:

"Well, I guess we can start the season. You're back, big guy." It doesn't matter that "Big Guy" is all of 5 foot 4 in his basketball sneakers. "Big Guy" is the name of every guy whose name you can't remember.

Then one day you get nabbed. A gentleman is walking toward you smiling a big smile and waving a big "Hello". He obviously knows you.....BY NAME! You think to yourself.....quick, what's his name? It's Jeff. No, Jack. Oh, he's getting closer. His wife is Ethel. He's a golfer. Then just as he gets to you and extends his hand.....you remember!!!!!

"Hi, Errol, good to see you. Did you have a good summer, Errol? And how's Ethel, Errol?"

You're so excited you can't stop saying, Errol. But wait a minute. He was ill when you left for the summer. What was his illness? Knees? No. Prostate? No. Cataracts? No. I'm embarrassed. How can I ask him how he feels? I can't remember his illness. What can I do? I'll probe.

"How are you feeling, Errol?"

"I'm feeling great!"

That didn't work. I'll have to probe further.

"Did you do anything exciting over the summer?"

"Well, I finally had my shoulder fixed."

Thank you, thank you, thank you, Errol.....whatever your last name is.

HEAT?
WHAT HEAT?

Two different populations inhabit South Florida. There are the "Snowflakes," who live here in the winter but head for cooler climes in the summer. Then there are the "Rounders," who love it here all year round. I have heard that many "Rounders" look forward to that time of year when the "Snowflakes" pack up their stuff, load their cars on to the trailer trucks and head out. This is nothing like the Hatfields and McCoys or the Democrats and Republicans, but at least for the summer, the Rounders like Florida all for themselves.

If you're a "Snowflake," you'll know what this is all about. When you come back each winter, you always have to sit through the same speech from the "Rounders." I call it their, "Summer Love Song." It's a hard sell spiel that goes something like this:

"Hey, Jack, good to see you again. How was your summer?"

"Fabulous. I love it here in the summer more than the winter. I wish it was summer here all year round."

"What's so great?

"Are you kidding? Restaurants? Walk right in. Movies and shows? Any seat in the house. Golf times? Not needed. Traffic jams? They went back north with you. This is a summer paradise. And the shopping! You don't have to find a salesperson. They find you!"

"You don't find it too hot down here?"

"It's just as hot where you are. We do everything we always do."

"It's not too hot for golf?"

"Are you kidding? The golf is great. We tee off by 7:00 and we're off the course by 8:30."

"Off by 8:30? Then what do you do?"

"Anything we want to. Everyplace is air conditioned. The stores. The malls. The restaurants. Your car. It's always 71 or 72 degrees wherever you go. It's like living in San Diego."

"So you stay inside."

"No. We travel and take trips. The middle of June we flew to California for two weeks to visit my daughter. Drove the coast from L.A. to Frisco. Beautiful country. We were home for a week and then we flew to Europe for a 3 week cruise around Greece and Italy."

"You must have come home exhausted."

Had no time for tired. We rented a house in Vermont for August. We love Vermont. On our way home, we took a week in New York. Did the whole "shop" and "show" routine. Then back to Florida to greet the winter—and you! Let's have dinner some night. We'll call you.

No wonder these "Rounders" love it here in the summer. They're not here.

(How long can I sit?)

HOW DEEP IS THE OCEAN? HOW LONG IS A BASEBALL GAME?

Football may have it's February Super Bowl. Basketball may have its "March Madness." But October belongs to baseball. It's baseball's golden moment. It's World Series time.

I've never understood why it's called the "World" Series. It's strictly an American affair. One thing I do know.....better plan on many hours in front of the TV if you plan on watching it. Yes, baseball has become a snail of a game.....dragging itself through 9 innings. Sometimes unbearably slow. Why is baseball so slow, you ask? I have 2 theories.

One problem is the advent of the bullpen. Where are the old pitching greats who used to go 9 innings. Today it could take 3 or 4 pitchers to finish a game. Changing pitchers in the excitement of a rally, while the stands are rockin' and rollin', is one of the great wet blankets in sports. It's something like a telephone call in the middle of sex.

The manager steps out of the dugout and slowly makes his way to the mound. He confers with the pitcher.....and confers.....and confers. He's stalling to give the reliever more time to warm up. Finally, he signals to the bullpen for the reliever to come in.

The reliever gathers up his jacket.....walks out of the bull pen (maybe 450 feet away), strolls leisurely across the out field and across the infield.....finally arriving at the mound. The manager hands him the ball, gives him the, "Go get 'em, Tiger" speech, pats him on the tush and then heads back to the dugout.

"Tiger" now goes through the "pitcher's ritual." Adjusts his pants, shirt and sleeves. Loosens his pitching arm with a couple of windmill rotations. (This after just having warmed up for 10 minutes.) Now he paws at the mound with his cleats to get it just the way he likes it. Next, he throws 6 or 7 warm up pitches. Finally, he's ready to go. But first the catcher comes out to discuss the signals they'll use. Finally, everybody's ready. Okay fans, it's back to the sex.

Not so fast, fans! The reliever pitches to one man and here comes the manager again. He wants a new pitcher for the next batter. Forget the sex.

There's another factor slowing the game.....velcro! Yes, good old sticky, rip-it-apart, press-it-together-again velcro. Most hitters today wear golf gloves at bat. The gloves are closed with a strip of velcro. Many hitters will step out of the batter's box frequently, sometimes as often as every pitch, and go through a compulsive routine. Rip open the velcro on the right glove and then reseal it tightly. Rip open the velcro on the left glove and then reseal it tightly.

Mr. Commissioner, baseball fans have better things to do than watch a $10 million-dollar-a-year super star stand there and play with his velcro like a little kid playing with their "Silly Putty." Mr. Commissioner, tempus fugit!

This compulsion to rip apart velcro is infesting baseball. Sports medicine doctors should be looking into the causes and cure for CVB—"Compulsive Velcro Behavior." I think a new rule is needed. You can't fidget with your velcro more than 3 times during any at bat.

Well, I finally figured out why they call baseball, "America's Pastime." Watching baseball does pass time. But I love it and watch it many a night.

It's my Ambien.

DAMN YANKEE!

Welcome to Fenway Park, home of the Boston Red Sox and their long suffering fandom, who waited decades to rejoice in a world championship.

Welcome to Fenway.....a stadium that has lived under the "Curse of the Bambino" for over 80 years.....since the day the Red Sox sold Babe Ruth to the Yankees in 1920. A curse the Red Sox finally exorcised with a world championship in 2004 and again in 2007.

Welcome to Fenway.....capital of the, "I Hate The Yankees Nation".....a nation so populous and far reaching, it spawned the hit Broadway musical, *Damn Yankees*.

Welcome to Fenway.....along with Yankee Stadium, home to one of the bitterest and nastiest rivalries in all of sports.....Red Sox vs. Yankees.

There have been many Yankee superstars through the years who have beaten the Red Sox and helped perpetuate the curse.....Lou Gherig, Joe DiMaggio, Mickey Mantle, Roger Maris. But for today's Red Sox fans, no Yankee superstar embodies and personifies that Yankee hate more than the present Yankee super-duper, superstar, Alex Rodriguez.....A-Rod for short.

A Yankee game in Fenway Park today is, first and foremost, a chance for Boston fans to come and show their #@*% for A-Rod. They come to jeer and boo him.....insult him.....vilify him. They come with signs and banners of derision. If he gets a hit there is silence. If he strikes out there is thunderous cheering. If he makes an error, they're delirious. And if he leaves the bases loaded with two out, that alone is worth the price of admission.

Why this focus on A-Rod? When A-Rod decided to leave the Texas Rangers and play elsewhere, he was hotly pursued by both the Yankees and Red Sox. Neither wanted him to play for the other. It was a battle of the checkbooks for the best player in baseball. There was a song in the musical, "Damn Yankees", that foretold the results of this battle. The song was about a devil of a temptress named, Lola. The words said it all.....*Whatever Lola Wants, Lola Gets.*

In real life, Lola became that damn owner of the damn Yankees, George Steinbrenner. He and Lola shared mottos—"Whatever George Wants, George Gets." He had assembled baseball's most expensive payroll and A-Rod was just another $120 million or so.

A few seasons ago, there was a Friday night game at Fenway against the Yankees. It doesn't get any better or louder or more raucous than that. The fans were ready. The A-Rod insults were flying. The signs and banners were hoisted high. The beer was flowing and it was like A-Rod had a target on his back. And then a magic moment happened. A-Rod was at his usual post at third base when a little foul pop up was hit his way. He moved to his right towards the stands and gloved it easily. Then in a magnanimous gesture of friendship, he tossed the ball to a young fan in the stands. A peace offering. Were there cheers from the Sox fans? No! Was there any sign they might be willing to forgive and forget? Forget it!

But the moment was not ended. The best was yet to come. In a quiet gesture that yelled and booed louder than the taunting mob of 40,000, the young fan stuck a dagger in A-Rod's heart.

He threw the ball back.

I want to say, "Poor A-Rod." But that's the last thing I can call him.

LIFE NEVER RUNS OUT OF HUMOR

HI, TECH

Today's hi tech world is a far cry from the world I grew up in. The big marvel I remember back then was the pop up toaster. How did it know the bread was toasted? What a difference a bunch of decades make. These are techy times and I am struggling to keep up. I'm just not high tech. I'm not even low tech. I'm no tech!

My wife is a "<u>no</u> techy," too. But she tries. She will buy a new space age coffee maker and read every word of the instructions before she even tries to brew a drop. She studies. I have no patience for instructions. Very often they read like this is the first thing the writer ever wrote in English. But we're trying to join this modern world.

We've had serious TV tech problems. We bought two Sony's for our bedroom.....a big one and a small one. The small one is for my wife who can't sleep without a TV playing in her headphones all night. When the Sony's arrived, I couldn't wait to see the picture. I turned on the big set and the picture was great. But so was the picture on the little set. They both went on! I turned off the big one and the little one went off, too. I tried turning the small set on and off with its own remote. You got it......the big set went on and off. We had two different remotes but both remotes worked both sets.

Important tech fact—all Sony remotes work all Sony TV's. You can't put two Sony's in the same room. It's like putting Rosie O'Donell and Donald Trump in the same room. I also found out it's true of every make TV.

120

So how did we solve our Sony problem? Ingenuity! We built a little mountain of pillows in the middle of our bed. We sneaked up on each set from behind the pillow pile so only one set got the signal. It was ingenious.....but a real pain in the bipper. This was no way to live.

We decided to go super tech! We bought a super-duper system with a single remote that could run our air conditioning, our hot water heater, our garage doors and our outdoor lighting in addition to operating both TV's independent of each other. We dismantled the pillow pile!

I can report the system works.....but not so simply. It took us 2 or 3 lessons to learn the basic operation. We are now in "graduate school" taking advanced lessons in how to record weeks in advance and play a DVD. We're hoping to graduate in two more weeks. We're also going to book the instructor for lessons next fall when we come back south and have totally forgotten how the hell any of this stuff works.

But this is not our only class. My wife is taking computer lessons on how to copy and paste, among other challenges. She just can't get the hang of this cute, little, tricky, techy trick. (Say that 3 times fast!) She's also taking lessons on how to buy on E-Bay. As soon as she learns, I'm going to take lessons on how to sell on E-Bay.

We have a wonderful guy at our car dealer who's teaching us how to operate our new car's sound system, air conditioning and most challenging of all, the navigation system. We started the navigation lessons in our driveway but now he's going out on the road with us, having us get to actual destinations. Next week he's going to give us an address 30 miles away. We're going to strike out alone and try to get there using only our navigation system. It's our first solo flight!

I'm considering buying a new Blackberry, which I have to stop calling a Blueberry, which makes me sound like a real doofus. I want "<u>2 lrn how 2 txt</u>". (Pretty god, huh?) I have large hands and my fingers can't work with those little keys. Instead of a Blackberry, they should bring out a Watermelon.

I've got to go now. My kids were just down to celebrate my wife's birthday. They took a lot of pictures which they sent me on my computer. I am now going to retrieve them. I hope I can get them before her next birthday.

"G" AS IN GNATS

Do you have an easy name for people to hear and spell? You're probably a Smith or Jones or Brown. Not so with me. The salesperson asks me my name and I say, "Bushell." They say, "Kushell?" "No, Bushell." They say, "Oh, Mushell." "No, **B**ushell." And so it goes.

And that's in person. It's much worse over the phone. Even worse when it's a cell phone. And if it's a cell phone with a bad connection, that's the worst. Wait a minute. There's an even worse worst. How about when you and the person on the other end come from different languages and each of you has trouble understanding the other.

So, I'm always spelling out my name.....B" as in "boy".....U" as in "up".....S" as in stick.....etc., etc. But one day I got bored. I have to go through 7 letters like I'm in kindergarten reciting my ABC's. I decided to be creative. Now I do "B" as in "bougainvillea".....U" as in unctuous.....S" as in "swarthy." Get the idea?

Well, if you always have to plod through your name, letter by boring letter, this is for you. I've prepared an exciting, titillating, stimulating alphabet list. Tear it out. Keep it by your phone or in your wallet and next time someone can't get your name right, dazzle them!

"A" as in amethyst

"B" as in b-r-r-r-r

"C" as in czar

"D" as in dwarf

"E" as in euthanasia

"F" as in foie gras

"G" as in grrrrr

"H" as in herbal

"I" as in icky

"J" as in jalapino

"K" as in knock kneed

"L" as in the abbreviation of pound

"M" as in m-m-m good

"N" as in the middle of TNT

"O" as in oomph

"P" as in psoriasis

"Q" as in querulous

"R" as in rhinoplasty

"S" as in shhhh

"T" as in tsk tsk

"U" as in unctuous

"V" as in vrooom (like a Ferrari)

"W" as in wrangler

"X" as in xenophobia

"Y" as in yoo-hoo

"Z" as in z-z-z-z (snore)

Okay all you Smiths, Joneses and Browns.....now aren't you sorry nobody ever asks you to spell out your name. And here are some more reasons to be sorry. "K" as in knockwurst or knickknack....."E" as in etcetera....."H" as in hors doeuvres....."T" as in tsunami.....and I'll end on "O" as in the end of igloo.

Folks, it's time you got rid of that "B" for bat, "C" for cat mentality. Graduate kindergarten! Spell out your name like you're a Ph.D..

That's "P" as in psssst!

CARRY LOTS
OF SINGLES

I must admit there are times I am confused, uncomfortable and unsure of myself when it comes to tipping. I'm a fairly sophisticated guy who's traveled far and wide, been around and rubbed some pretty important elbows at some very "in" places. But there's a side of me that's a little small townish and it shows at certain tipping times.

Like the car wash. Your car goes in one end and comes out the other. There are guys at both ends expecting tips. Now tell me.....do you tip the guys at the entrance who hose down your wheels? And how much? And if you do, do you give the guys who wipe down your car at the other end, less than you would have given, if you hadn't tipped at the first end? Better yet.....is this all academic because they share their tips?

And let's be totally honest with each other. Do you tip by socio-economic car? Should a BMW or Benz owner give more than a Chevy or Ford owner? Do the car washers expect it? And what do they expect from a Bentley owner? This is why I don't own a Bentley.

Okay, so you tipped your way through the car wash and you're on your way to get something to eat. But you're in a hurry, so you stop for a sandwich to go. It comes out and you go to pay. It's decision time. They always have a little jar at the cash register. Some say, "Tips." Some just say, "Thanks." And some say nothing. But you can't miss the jar because it always has money stuffed in it. That's to make you feel like all the "to go" customers are tipping.

Besides, I'm savvy enough to know most of the money in that jar is theirs. They're shaming me into a tip. And most of the time.....I'm shamed.

I'm also not a good giver of tips. I just hand it over for all to see. There are some who deliver their tip with great flair and style. They "slip" their tip. Next time you're at an elegant restaurant, watch the captain. He gets tipped big time. Yes, men will pay a lot to be personally greeted by the captain and shown right to their table. Yes, "their" table.

For this the captain doesn't just get tipped. He gets shmeared. Ah, the shmear.....to cover with money.....like you shmear paint across a wall or cream cheese across a bagel. You shmear money across the palm.

But what makes the shmear so outstanding is the delivery. You must shmear with a flair. Let's watch a video tape of the perfect shmear. Notice, as the shmearer enters the restaurant and approaches the captain, he has the shmear perfectly positioned between his thumb and fingertips. Now, as he passes the captain, shmear arm fully extended, the captain drops his receiving hand, opens his fingers thus giving the shmnearer a big open palm target.

Okay, now stop the tape. This is the perfect shmear position. Shmearer and shmearee both have arms fully extended to the same height. Shmearee's hand open, palm exposed. Then with the timing of an NFL quarterback and the slick of a prestidigitator, the shmearer hands off.....no he just slides the shmear into the shmearee's waiting palm and keeps walking. The captain gracefully closes his fingers around the shmear. It is now his. He slides it into his shmear pocket never looking to see if it's a 10 or 20. (The usual shmear.) Neither man ever looked down. It takes only a millisecond but when done right, it is an art form.

I'm not ready for the shmear. I'm still trying to figure out who and what to tip at the car wash and whether to leave a tip in that little glass jar for my tuna to go.

Got any tips?

SAILING, SALE-ING

Vacation Report

I'm talking to you from the high seas—cruising historic ports on the Aegean. (What a great crossword puzzle word!) This is a cruising day. No new port to visit. I thought this would be a good time to talk to you because I'm not eating. A rare moment. These cruises boldly promise, "All You Can Eat!" Judging by the bodies walking by me, I would say these people don't take that promise as an inducement. They take it as a challenge. They're out to show the cruise line—"All They Can Eat!"

This is especially true at dinner. The reason dinner is such a gluttonous affair is simple. You have to have a real substantial dinner to sustain you til the midnight buffet. I can feel the excitement growing as the next meal approaches.

I must admit I'm homesick. I miss my kids and grandchildren. I miss my bed. I even miss my time zone. But the ship is beautiful and the service warm and courteous. I'll give you an example. Some friends of mine aboard got the most wonderful compliment from their chambermaid. She told them they keep the neatest room on the ship. They were so proud. Now they find themselves constantly cleaning and straightening up the room—for the chambermaid. They have an image to live up to. (Beware the oldest chambermaid trick on the high seas!)

The big question on these cruising days is what to do? You can always play shuffleboard—but I'm too young to play shuffleboard.

Cards are popular—especially bridge. When it comes to bridge, I'm out to sea. I would play ping pong but there are no ball boys. There's an art auction at 2 but my wife has told me all our money is for shopping. Actually, a day like this is a blessed relief. I don't have to go shopping. And that means I don't have to bargain. Yes, cruising is bargaining warfare—Euro combat!

I've been at it every day and I'm exhausted. It's like a boxing match. You and the merchant put on the gloves and bargain it out. This takes strength and stamina. He fights this fight a hundred times a day. *And he's undefeated*! That is, until you!

After all, what does he know that you don't? So he knows the exact karat count—the quality of the diamonds—the color of the gems—the weight of the gold—none of which you know. But you have an advantage. He's alone in the ring while you have a manager, a handler in your corner to advise you and urge you on—who won't let you quit til the other guy is beaten and bloodied. You have your wife!

They say the best deal is when both parties walk away happy. This is that kind of deal. You walk away thinking you got it for a steal. He walks away knowing he got a price he never thought anyone would pay him.

If you ever knew, you'd eat your heart out.

But not before dinner.

S-H-H-H-H-H

May I tell you about my other love. Ahhhh, my passion! She does for me what no one else can do. I meet with her and I am young again..... rejuvenated.....reborn! Under her spell, my cares and worries fly far, far away. Our time together is rapturous. I treasure it.

Every afternoon my love and I rendezvous far from any inquisitive eyes. We lie together blissfully. We are alone. This is our time. She wraps me in her arms and I drift away into another world.....I am in a dream. We come together so joyfully.....and part so regretfully. We have been meeting like this for years. I speak, of course, about those rapturous afternoon moments when I rendezvous with my dearest, my love.....my nap.

My nightly sleep is fulfilling and necessary but my afternoon nap is delicious. She comes unannounced. She sneaks up on me. I just let myself go and she takes me.

To go to sleep takes preparation. Go to my bedroom. Get undressed. Take care of my nightly bathroom chores. Turn off the lights.

To go to nap takes no preparation. Leave the TV on. Let the newspaper or book rest on your chest. Don't touch your glasses. Pillows not necessary. Stay sprawled on the couch. My nap beckons: "Come as you are. Let me take you away. And snore if you like. We're alone."

Sleep is fine.....but snoozing is divine. Sometimes I think just 20 minutes of snooze does more for me than a night of Z-Z-Z-Z-Z.

Nothing could ever come between me and my nap. Except one. I speak of that damn machine.....that loud, blaring ring of the telephone. I'm jolted and jarred! My nap lets go of me gently.....slowly I come back to the world of awake. Shakespeare was right....."Parting is such sweet sorrow." The phone rings again. My nap must finally let me go. We bid adieu.....until tomorrow.

I pick up the phone. I bark, "HELLO!" Yes, I'm perturbed. No, the caller is not trying to sell me something. Nor is the caller doing a survey. It's worse.

It's for my wife!

HONOR THY MOTHER, FATHER AND MY 7:30 RESERVATION

So you're going out to dinner. You've got a 7:30 reservation and you're hungry. What are the odds that when you walk into that restaurant at 7:30, the hostess will greet you, "Good evening. Your table and waiter are waiting. Follow me."

Forget it! It never happens. What happens is the hostess flashes you a lovely smile and says, "Your table will be ready shortly. Why don't you sit at the bar and we'll call you."

Funny thing is, she already called me.....yesterday.....to confirm my 7:30 reservation. She knew I was coming at 7:30. She knew I was coming hungry. When they call the day before, they should say, "I'm calling to confirm your reservation for 4 tomorrow night at sometime after 7:30." That might defuse things a bit.

There is a way to handle this situation. When she tells you to wait at the bar.....DON'T GO! Don't budge. Stand tall right up against her desk and HOVER! HOVER! HOVER! Invade her territory. Let her know you're protecting your position on her list.

An important hovering fact: tall guys make better hoverers than short guys. Short guys will hover <u>at</u> the hostess but tall guys will hover <u>over</u> her.....as in, "The helicopter hovered overhead." But hovering is getting harder. The IHGSU—the *International Hostess' Greet and Seat Union*" has been complaining to restaurant owners about this hovering harassment. Restaurant owners are now hiring taller hostesses. It's hard to hover over a hostess who's hovering over you. I have no advice for those times you get out hovered.

I do have advice if you are dining out with other couples. Before you get to the restaurant, appoint a DH....."Designated Hoverer." This way the NH's (non-hoverers) can relax at the bar and enjoy a drink knowing their interests are being hovered over.

To hover well, you must stand tall. Lean over a bit at the waist, so you are intruding further into the hostess' space. In no time, you will become a nuisance. You will move to the top of her "get rid of" list. As the dinner crowd piles in, and as she tells more and more people to step aside and wait at the bar, other hoverers will try to take over your spot. Stand your ground. Hover strong.

It is a proven fact.....a hostess will leave those who are waiting at the bar.....waiting at the bar. She will get rid of the pests first. Said another way: "HE WHO HOVERS.....GETS VIBRATED FIRST!"

And when you finally get seated, enjoy your meal. Just hope the hostess doesn't give you one of those over attentive, obsequious waiters who will hover over <u>you</u> all night.

Hostesses have been known to hover back!

IT'S CHRISTMAS.
OPEN THE SOFA BEDS.

"I'm the happiest grandma in America. My son just called with great news—he's coming down with the whole family for a week. I'm so excited. When I meet them at the airport, the little ones will run up and give me big hugs and kisses....."Grandma! Grandma!" They're so cute, so adorable. Is there any joy in life more joyous?

So tell me.....how come after 2 days, I can't wait for them to leave?

The mess they make. My son comes for a week and doesn't unpack. He lives out of a suitcase right in the middle of the floor. Do I have to tell you what I spent for big, built-ins with enough draws so they could stay a month. (God forbid!) And the special Italian hardware I had to wait weeks for so the draws would gl-i-i-i-i-de open. My son has never felt that gli-i-i-i-de. What's worse, none of this bothers my daughter-in-law. But that's another story.

Of course the little ones learn from their father. They put everything away in this one giant draw. It's called the floor! The floors are littered with underwear, wet bathing suits, socks, sneakers, crumpled shirts, golf clubs. Yesterday, my husband tripped over a wet towel the kids left right in the middle of the floor. He picked himself up....<u>but not the towel</u>! He left it for the next tripper. I told my husband, "Somebody has to teach these kids responsibility, neatness, respect." You know what he said to me....."Look at your son."

Of course, my daughter-in-law pretends not to see the mess. I see it, so I walk out the back door of my house and around to the front just to get to the garage. Just so I don't have to see their rooms.

But their rooms are not the real mess. You want to talk mess? Step into my kitchen and onto my beautiful Mexican tile floor. But be careful. Don't step on any peanut butter or jelly or pancakes or pasta or baloney or Cheerios. And watch out for grape juice puddles. And don't get your foot stuck in maple syrup. I don't think anyone in my family knows where their mouth is. A homeless family could eat very nicely off my kitchen floor. And gain weight!

My husband notices none of this. Someone explain to me, how can you step on a Cheerio......on a tile floor.....barefoot.....and not know you stepped on something? That's my husband. But he was right about one thing in the kitchen. I should have gone with linoleum.

And you never have enough food. I have to shop 3 or 4 times while they're here so I won't run out of food for the floor. And it's not just me. Last year at the supermarket, I saw this cart coming down the aisle loaded to the top with food. A little old grandma was pushing it and muttering, "Only 2 more days—2 more days."

Worse than the mess is the noise. The phones ringing.....the TV's blaring.....the cartoons.....the video games.....the kids whining and crying. I think they have a meeting every night: "Tomorrow you whine, Michael, and I'll cry."

But the worst noise is that never ending, "HOCKETA-POCKETA." Morning, noon and night pounding in my head: "HOCKETA POCKETA." You know that noise. The washing machine and dryer. They're always HOCKETING POCKETING. Last year I picked up the family at the airport, and when we got home, I right away made them some lunch. While I'm making delicious, I hear that HOCKETA POCKETA starting. How can that be? They just got here. Would you believe it? They brought their dirty laundry down with them.

You'd think my kids walked around spotless. They don't. They look like slobs! <u>Cute</u> slobs! So what is my daughter-in-law always washing? I'll tell you what—towels!!!!! You'd think I was running a Turkish steam bath. Did Congress pass a law you can't use a towel twice?

I hate to bring up money but it's very expensive when they come down. I turn on the pool heater 3 days before they get here. I want the water nice and toasty warm so they should swim a lot. It's the only time anybody uses our pool. No matter how early I start the heater, no matter how warm I make the pool, it's never warm enough for my daughter-in-law. She likes it like a spa. My husband says, "Let her take a hot bath."

I always, make sure to kid-proof the house before they come. I put away anything that's breakable, valuable, delicate, beautiful, sensitive, carved, sentimental, fine or pretty to look at. I also put sheets over all the furniture and take down all the art. My house is now decorated in what I would call......neo-barren. My husband came home and thought the painters were coming. Maybe I'll have them come as long as I'm ready.

Well, before you know it, I'll be taking them back to the airport. By the time I drive home, I'll be missing them. Can you believe it! I'll miss the noise, the mess, the crying and whining. And the most unbelievable thing......I'll start looking forward to their next visit.

"Are we crazy?"

DON'T RETIRE TIL YOU READ THIS

This is for all you men who are nearing retirement. Retirement can be a scary thought. I know what you're thinking. "What am I going to do with the rest of my life? How much golf and cards can I play? How many books can I read?" Well, here are some tips on what to expect and how to handle your new life.

First, you must understand that all your business life you have been a real go-getter.....a super achiever. First one in the office every morning.....last one to leave at night. You have been driven to build your business bigger and bigger. Work. Work. Work. Yes, you have been a....."Man On A Mission!"

Well, guys, once you retire, no more, "Man On A Mission." Now you're a, "MAN ON AN ERRAND!"

Errands, guys, that's your new life. Running errands is what will keep you spry and young. But listen closely.....there's a very scientific way you must run your errands. <u>Don't run</u>. Don't rush. Take them slowly. Drag them out. Pad them. Make them last longer than they really have to. Make them seem more important then they really are. We call this, "Much Ado About Nothing." Let me give you an example.

One of your most frequent errands is going to be the cleaners. Your wife will be after you constantly, "Honey, you have to take in the cleaning. Honey, you have to pick up the cleaning. Honey, take in. Honey, pick up." Now listen very closely. <u>Here's the secret of retirement</u>

in a nut shell. *You never take in.....and pick up.....on the same trip.* That's two separate errands. You've killed twice the time. That's "Much Ado About Nothing."

Another frequent errand that will keep your motor running—grocery shopping. Now the supermarket can be a very confusing place to someone like you who has rarely shopped alone. Maybe never even shopped! I can see you wandering up and down the aisles looking for your Metamucil, your Bran Flakes, your Preparation H. I'll save you lots of time and trouble. I'll give you a tip right now. The prunes are in "Dried Fruits".....next to the raisins.

Now I have to be perfectly honest with you guys. There will be days when you have no errands. Don't despair. Don't fret. Because on those days you will have a very important job. You will be the "waiter." Yes, you wait for the cable guy. You wait for the carpet cleaner guy.....you wait for any guy coming.

You will immediately ask, "Okay, I'll wait but when are they coming?" Don't bother calling. I'll tell you right now when they're coming. They'll be there sometime between 11 and 4. To which you say, "That's ridiculous. I have to sit around all day." To which I say, "You got something better to do?"

Hopefully all the workmen will have come and gone by 4 because at 4 you enter the......"Nap Zone." This is a retiree ritual and very much needed. Those errands can knock you out. And besides you have to rest up for the next retiree ritual.....dinner out. No more home cooking because your wife has also retired. But dinners out are great. Good food with good friends. Only one thing you have to worry about. Just hope and pray nobody asks you, "What did you do today, Jack?"

You're going to love retirement, guys. See you at the post office—the cleaners—and I'll definitely see you in "Dried Fruits".

ON AN UPPER

How many times have you done something silly or just plain stupid and then muttered to yourself, "Why did I do that?" We all have these "why" moments. I seem to be having them more and more often. I'll give you an example of me at my "why" worst.

Let me set the scene. I'm walking through a hotel lobby on my way to the 16th floor. I walk up to a bank of elevators where a group of people are waiting for an "UP" lift. (That's English talk, not spiritual!) Acting purely on habit, I go to press the "UP" button. But just as my finger gets there, I stop. It's already lit. I've been beaten to the press.

So what should I do? I should retreat. The elevator has already been summoned. No need to re-press. Well, maybe <u>you</u> don't have to re-press but I must! I can't repress my need to re-press. Only after <u>I</u> press, do I know for sure the elevator got the message. What is this compulsion? It's become my credo.....never trust a pressed button. And that goes for "UP" or "DOWN."

So my compulsive side wins again. I re-press! Now I think to myself, "Why did I do that?" The original presser, lurking somewhere behind me, probably hates me. He's thinking, "Who does this guy think he is.....Super Presser? I'm not good enough to get the elevator? Does he think the elevator ignores me and only listens to him?"

I step back, making sure I keep my back to the crowd so I won't get any nasty looks. While I wait there with my "UP" mates, a lady walks over and without any hesitation, she marches right up to the button and presses it. She's so casual. She saw the light was already lit. Did she care that she repressed my re-press? Not a bit! So I am not alone. There are other compulsive re-pressers out there. I wonder, is this obsessive button behavior common?

Despite all this pressing, the elevator doesn't come. I'm in a hurry. I'm edgy. It's time to let the elevator know I'm perturbed and impatient. It's re-re-press time.

But now I must talk to the elevator in a different tone of voice..... a sterner tone. No more, "Mr. Nice Guy." This time it's not just a nice press. This time I JAB! JAB! JAB! that button. My jabs are rapid and staccato like. All the impatience in me is now flowing out through my rigid, stiffened forefinger.....into the button.....and up to the elevator. The message is loud and clear. "Listen here, Mr. Otis, you get yourself down here. Fast!"

It's an impressive display. I sense that my "Up" mates stand in awe. They have found their leader.....their spokesman. They have put their "Up" fate in my hands. I am now their "DP"....."Designated Presser." The original presser is all but forgotten.

When the elevator finally comes, (two usually come at the same time), I join the press of people and enter my "UP" lift. I'm shoved into a corner unable to see the bank of buttons. I can't press my floor. So I politely ask someone to please press #16.

And then it happens. The entire elevator turns and faces me. In unison they let me know—

"16 is already pressed!" (There is an unspoken, "Sir," in their tone.)

I thank them. When we get to #16, just a little old lady and I are left. I follow her out the door. As I pass the bank of buttons, I take one more shot. I press #35.

Why did I do that?

WHERE D'YA WANNA?

Retirement is truly the great escape from the pressures and stress of business. No more running around and flying around from meeting to meeting. Gone is that "oval office" pressure—the weighty decisions that you and you alone had to make: overhead—inventory—bottom line—expansion—hire—fire—taxes.

Now that you're retired, you are a new man—carefree and decision free. Well, not quite. There are still decisions you must make.

Nine iron or wedge?

Throw the king or the jack?

Order chicken or steak?

And then there is the weighty decision that is laid upon you every morning—as soon as you get up—the moment you open your eyes. Your wife has to know—

"Where d'ya wanna eat tonight?"

"I don't care. Wherever you wanna eat."

"I have no preferences."

"Neither do I. Wherever you wanna eat is fine."

"Well, what kind of food do you want?"

"It's hard for me to know what I want for dinner at 8 o'clock in the morning."

"Well, you have to know. We have to make a reservation or we won't get in anywhere."

"I'll eat wherever you want."

"I'll tell you what—we have a date with Alice and Bob. Call them and see where they want to eat. I have to go the gym."

So you call Alice.

"Hi, Alice. Listen we have a date tonight. Where d'ya wanna eat?"

"Anywhere you wanna eat."

"Well, any place is all right with us, too. Pick one."

"I would be happy eating anywhere."

"Anywhere's closed tonight. Ask, Bob, where he wants to eat." (She yells into the other room) "Bob, it's Gordon. Where d'ya wanna eat tonight? (A PAUSE) He said he'll eat anywhere you wanna eat."

"How about Chinese food. We could go to Mao Tse Tung's on Federal."

"That's not good. I got sick last week on Moo Goo something."

"Well, what kind of food would you like; steaks, Italian, Asian, deli?"

"Anything as long as it's cooked."

"Hold on Alice. It's Betty on the other line—Hi, honey. Yes, I called Alice. I'm on the phone with her right now.....no, I haven't made a reservation yet....yes, I asked her....she'll eat anywhere we wanna eat. Yes, she asked, Bob. He'll eat anywhere we wanna eat. He doesn't care. We're all agreeable to any place. So, honey, this is where we stand at this moment.....anyone'll eat anywhere anyone wants to eat. We're at a standstill. We're not going anywhere. We have eat lock! Got any suggestions? Okay, that sounds good—I'll suggest it. Hold on—"

"Alice, Betty suggested a salad place."

"I like that. I'm sick of stuffing myself. Where's a good salad place?"

"I don't know. I never eat salads."

"If you'd rather not have a salad, we'll eat anywhere you wanna eat."

We interrupt this conversation for the sake of sanity. And you thought your business decisions were tough.

P. S. I'm going to open a restaurant called, "Anywhere You Wanna Eat." It's got great word-of-mouth built in.

OH, THE MEMORIES I'VE FORGOTTEN

Doctors tell us we have two forms of memory.....short term and long term. We can remember things and events from long ago but we can draw a total blank on recent events. Very recent! Like whom you played golf with yesterday. We can forget even more recently than yesterday. "Why did I just walk into this room?"

We can even forget just seconds ago—

"Did I just take my pills?"

So let's forget the forgotten and spend some joyful time remembering things we can recall. Let's take a stroll down "Memory Lane." Follow me.

Remember when the most you could win was $64,000?

Remember when the only billionaires were countries?

Remember when we all drank water from a faucet? Remember the milkman and the coal man? And who could forget the grocer who pulled out a little, stub-of-a-pencil from behind his ear and figured your bill on the back of a bag (Brown paper). The bag was your only receipt.

Remember the Nash, the Hudson and the car that looked like it was going forward and backwards at the same time? The Studebaker. Remember the car Ford would like to forget? Did you ever actually see a Delorean? I miss whitewalls and running boards. Loved those rumble seats.

Remember when you couldn't sleep at night so you turned on your TV and watched test patterns. What set did you have? A Dumont or a Philco? Remember black and white TV and rabbit ears? Remember snow? Remember the magnifying glass you put in front of the screen to make the picture bigger? And everybody had to sit single file so you wouldn't get distortion. And remember when you had to get up to change channels? Couldn't do it today.

Remember when we used to go to the movies and sit through a double feature plus a newsreel plus coming attractions plus a serial? All for 25 cents and 5 cent candy. How did we sit for so long? They must have had an intermission or else when did we go? Ooops.....I forgot. We didn't have to go back then. And by the way, whatever happened to ushers?

Okay, folks, let's stroll a little faster. Do you remember fluoroscopes—fireside chats—hot pants—Kilroy was here—the Toni Twins—Green stamps—phonographs—Esso—"In Like Flynn"—the "March Of Dimes"—that scary twosome Peter Lorre and Sidney Greenstreet—zoot suits—Uncle Miltie and his super pitchman, Sid ("Tell Ya' What I'm Gonna Do") Stone—victory gardens—"Good night, Mrs. Calabash"—the Automat—Adler Elevator Shoes—"What's My Line?"—Smoke rings in Times Square—labor strikes—Gimbels—"President" Dewey—bobby socks—the Dionne 5—Newsreels—Alfred Hitchcock at the Bates Motel—Dodgers from Brooklyn—Major Bowes—the Flying Tigers—Masters and Johnson—Chesterfields—Betty Grable's legs—Rita Hayworth's bedroom picture in "Life"—pin ups—victory gardens and victory bonds—"Loose Lips Sink Ships"—VJ Day and that big smooch in Times Square—The Saturday Evening Post—Allen's Alley and Senator Claghorn—and then to close out every year and usher in a new one, we kissed to Guy Lombardo's "Auld Ang Syne."

I hope you enjoyed our little stroll down Memory Lane. I'm sorry I have to quit.....but my hip is starting to hurt.

FIT FITS!

Some of us are good at golf. Some of us excel in tennis. Some of us win at bridge. But there's one activity we're <u>all</u> super stars at.....eating!

We're snackers! Nibblers! Noshers! Buffet lovers! We eat out every day that ends in a "Y". We order every course and side dish that come with the dinner. Why not? They come with the dinner! You have to take them. We try to be good with desserts. We order one treat for the table with 4 spoons. Then we hog half of it. If there's anything we can't finish, we take it home in a doggy bag. Except, <u>we're</u> the doggy!

This feeding frenzy has left us in a state of frustration which can be described poignantly in two dreaded words.....two words that are uttered in disgust and frustration in virtually every bedroom in America. You probably have uttered.....no, screamed.....these very words yourself....."**NOTHING FITS!**"

Indeed, we are a people that nothing fits. Can you hear yourself: "This is a disaster! How did this happen to me? I could scream! Nothing fits! I must go on a diet. I have nothing to wear." America, have we reached a point where a woman would sooner reveal her age than her size?

What to do? Don't run to the tailor. Without looking, I can tell you there's nothing left to let out. You went through that long ago. Even scarier, this is your "fat" wardrobe and it doesn't fit. And, of course, your Adonis ego won't let you go up another size. "There's no way I'm a 40. These pants are mis-marked!"

So we fight to make it fit. Oh the struggle.....the pulling and tugging.....the wrenching......the sucking in, in, in.....and just when you think there's not another suck left in you, you reach down to your toes and bring up a suck like you've never sucked it up before.

Eureka! "We have a fit, Houston!"

Such a valiant struggle to make 36 inches go around 40. Such a struggle deserves a paean, an ode to all us battlers of the bulge. I have such an ode. So, with all due respect to Mr. Shelley and his immortal, "*Ode To A Grecian Urn*," here is my "*Ode To Our Pots*".....as in potbellies.

> *Every day I'm getting more and more depressed*
> *Every day it's getting harder to get dressed*
> *Oh, it really does astound me*
> *How my clothes don't go around me*
> *It's a crime.....it's the pits.....Nothing Fits!*
>
> *When I have to pick an outfit here's my plight*
> *Every outfit fits me snug or fits me tight*
> *Gonna live on fruit and juices*
> *I just wanna feel what loose is*
> *Hear me cry.....I could die.....Nothing Fits!*
>
> *Oh, I have a tire and it makes me fat*
> *Every day I pray my tire will go flat*
> *Oh, you really know it's there, folks*
> *Cause I also have a spare, folks*
> *Hear me moan.....hear me groan.....Nothing Fits!*
>
> *Yes, the styles today are all designer chic*
> *So you better have a figure that is sleek*
> *If you lunch on hot pastrami*
> *Just forget about Armani*
> *Georgio is a no.....he won't fit!*

Have you heard about the pants that will expand
It's the fabric that they're using in the band
So I let myself to hell go
Now I'm running out of velcro
It's the worst....I am cursed....Nothing Fits!

Every night we get so happy we could shout
It's the one time we can let it all hang out
Every night before we doze off
We can finally ri-i-i-p our clothes off!
It's a joy...it's the best....WE'RE UNDRESSED!!!!!

YOU WANT TO SIT WHERE???

I know you're not reading this sitting in your living room. I know because you <u>never</u> sit in your living room. Why do we still build living rooms? Why do we call them "living" rooms? We don't "live" in them. We don't even sit in them, chat in them or gather in them. We just look in and admire them as we walk by. Yes, these are our "Look In" rooms.

The cushions and pillows are always plumped up perfect. It's so tempting to just plop into that plump. And one day, if somebody should, as soon as they get up, you run to re-plump. This room is no place for butt impressions. This room must always be plump perfect.

To further preserve and protect their "Look In" room, many wrap it in plastic.....a kind of "saran wrap" for sofas and chairs. I can tell you first hand, when you sit in a "saraned" seat, a lot of the soft, whoosh goes out of the cushion when there's plastic between you and the plump. I know. My mother "saraned" almost everything.

Yes, our "Look In" room is beautiful to behold. But don't get too close. Just look in. It's almost as though we had a thick red velvet rope across the entrance. You can see we spent a fortune on our "Look In" room. Decorator done! (You can see it, can't you?) Of course, when your grandchildren come down, it's the, "DON'T EVEN LOOK!" room.

And when you entertain new friends, you always stop at your "Look In" room for a brief showing.

"Oh, darling, this room is so elegant and fine it belongs in Architectural Digest."

"Im so glad you like it. Come let's adjourn to the den for some drinks and hors d'oeuvres."

And so it sits—alone in solitary refinement—yearning for a friendly tush to come plop in its plump.

And then comes the shocker. One day the lady of the house suggests the inexplicable.....the preposterous.....the unbelievable!

"Honey, I think our "Look In" room needs redoing."

The man is shocked. "Redoing? For what? It's never been used. It's been dusted and vacuumed to death. It's probably the cleanest, most sanitary room in the house. Our furniture is as new as any new furniture we're going to buy. It has no mileage on it! Is there something I don't see? Are the pillows and cushions un-plumping? Do we have "sofa sag?" Is the furniture or carpeting faded? Impossible! The sun is not allowed in this room. Our curtains and drapes are impregnable. And they're always drawn.

"No, it's not that, dear. It's just old. It's not today's look. Honey, this is our 'Look In' room. It's whole purpose is to have the right look so when people look in they say, 'Beautiful'—'Gorgeous'—'Drop Dead!' You don't want a 'Look In' room that nobody wants to look in."

"I give up. Call the decorator. But this time we give her a budget." (It doesn't help!)

Of course no discussion of this room you never sit in would be complete without a mention of its nearby neighbor.....your dining room.....the room you never dine in.

JUNK

When we bought our first house in Florida, we were thrilled. It was the perfect size and had virtually everything we needed. It never occurred to us we had everything except the one thing we needed most.....a basement. We had no place to dump things.....throw things.....accumulate things. Everybody needs some place for all the junk they collect and just can't get themselves to throw away. Since they don't build basements down here, I guess they build the next best thing.....storage places.....lots of storage places.

Know this and never forget it.....once you put your junk in a storage area, it never comes out! It's your junk and your storage area for life. The reason is simple.....there's no place to throw the stuff away. The storage area won't let you get rid of it anywhere on their property. If they did, it would become their junk. So where can you dump.....excuse me.....leave the stuff? Should I take it to some far off, isolated, wooded spot, known only to serial killers. I think not.

And you never see the problem coming. You rent storage space as a temporary measure. You think you'll need the space for maybe a year. After three years of paying rent, it dawns on you.....you're in for life! And your kids' life! And their kids' life! This junk will be in your family in perpetuity!

Sometimes I have to go to my space with a new piece of junk I can't get myself to throw out. I walk through the place and it's loaded with other people's junk just like mine. Their bins are full. They're in for life just like me. We're all prisoners.....lifers! This is a cell block for junk. And guards are not needed because nobody's going to try to steal your stuff. Who wants <u>your</u> junk? There's no escape.

Now here's the kicker. I also rent storage space up North. We moved from a large house to a small apartment and just couldn't get ourselves to throw anything away. I'm a two time lifer.

I keep hearing these politicians warn we are going to strap future generations with our huge national debt. Worse than that, I'm going to stick my future descendants with two storage areas of junk they can't use.....they don't want.....and they can't get rid of. How does that make me feel? Like junk!

My wife and I decided to visit our lawyer and make provisions in our wills for the passing on of our storage junk. This must be treated like a family safe deposit box. We are going to leave everything to our children equally so there will be no fighting or jealousy over our junk. But it's unfair to stick our kids with the responsibility and expense of maintaining and caring for our junk. To that end, we plan to establish and endow a trust fund in the name of, *The Bushell Junk Storage Complex.* Our children will be named Executors and Trustees of this fund and will be directed to act wisely and prudently in safeguarding the principle and to always, first and foremost, invest in the best interests of our junk.

Only one proviso. No junk bonds.

SHORT THOUGHTS

Have you watched these big million dollar poker tournaments on TV? It's pure Vegas. They call the game, "Texas Hold 'Em." Funny thing is, the first time I heard them talking about "Texas Hold 'Em".....I thought it was a new immigration law

****

With all the great song writers out there, we don't have a ballad for today. Nobody's written a love song in tune with this computerized, digitalized, pod-ized world we live in. I have the perfect song.....the first love song of the 21st Century. It's warm. It's cuddly. It's cute. It's so singable.

I'll give you the title....."I Wanna Be Your Laptop."

****

Do you know any poor millionaires? That's not an oxymoron. I know quite a few of these types. They've got scads of money but it kills them to spend it. They fly economy. They're tight tippers. They wait for sales. They'll park three blocks away to avoid the valet. I have my own little phrase to describe these types. I recently told one of them....

"Ralph, it's a waste of money for you to be rich."

****

You're out to dinner at a fancy restaurant. You've been waiting 20 minutes for a table. In walks a couple. The maitre d' runs to greet them.

"Ah, good evening, Mr. Stewart. Your table is waiting." Let me tell you, folks, Mr. Stewart pays plenty for that "recognition". I, on the other hand, am a totally unknown diner. Not a single maitre d' or hostess or waiter or waitress or bar tender or bus boy or valet knows my name.

But I have my moment of fame—a place where I am known, instantly recognized and fawned over. Walgreens prescriptions. I walk in to pick up my latest medicine and I get the royal greeting. "Hello, Mr. Bushell. Good to see you again, Mr. Bushell. How are those new pills working?"

Let me tell you, folks, the insurance company and I pay plenty for this recognition.

****

This was related to me by some friends who were flying from Denver to Aspen. As they approached the landing, the stewardess got on the PA to make the following announcement:

"We'll be landing in Aspen in a few minutes. I hope you enjoyed the flight despite the turbulence. Please be careful when you open the luggage bin above you. Shift happens."

True story. No shift!

****

May I tell you a grandchild story. Just one. This one came from the mouth of my 4 year old grandson. He loves animal shows. One night he came running out of his room all excited, "Daddy, daddy, Jeff Corwin is going to be on TV this Sunday night with the lions and tigers of Africa."

"That's great. Did they say what time?"

"It's on at 8, 7 Central."

You just can't write stuff like that.

****

I love the retired lifestyle. It's so simple. My closet is so uncluttered. Gone are all those business suits and shirts and ties and dress shoes. It's so easy now. All I need is a sport jacket for dinner—a blue suit for weddings—and a black suit for funerals.

I'm perfectly suited for retirement.

****

I have for you today the perfect definition of "gauche." I had a gauche client. He avoided anything cultural and had no time or taste for art. He had to make a business trip to Paris. His wife begged him to visit the Louvre and see the "Mona Lisa". It was an image he would never forget.

Well, he found free time and surprisingly, hopped in a cab and headed for the Louvre. When he got there, he ran in to see "Mona". And I mean ran. He told the cabbie to wait.

Tres gauche!

****

Do you find it hard to open a lot of today's products. Manufacturers are locking us out. Take good, old Corn Flakes. The box opens easily. But to get to the corn flakes you have to open the plastic bag inside. So I grab it with my thumbs and forefingers and pull.....and tug.....and tear. I can't get to the corn flakes. This bag is super sealed. I'm getting frustrated. I'm getting angry. I'm desperate.

"Okay, little plastic bag. I'll show you who's boss." I grab a kitchen knife and stab the bag. I stab and stab and stab. I'm mad. Wait a minute. Does this make me a cereal killer?

****

Here's one for the books. We were flying Alitalia in Italy. I got 2 nonsmoking seats. Shortly after takeoff, the gentleman directly across the aisle from me lit up a cigarette. I was engulfed in his exhale. I called the stewardess over and politely reminded her, "Miss, we're supposed to have two non smoking seats." She politely replied, "That's what you have. Your side is non smoking. The other side of the aisle is smoking."

Who figured this out? What were they smoking?

****

While driving the other day, I passed a new phenomenon on the road. At least for me it was new. At first I thought it was an SUV. It had that big, wide body silhouette. As I passed it, I realized it had a small, open flat bed in the rear—like a truck. It was part SUV and part truck.

Detroit, you made a, "Suck!"

****

There are certain people I find a real turn off....the hoity-toities. They're so socially superior. Example: three ladies at an elegant cocktail gathering talking about an exciting new musical coming to Broadway.....

"I heard it's another, 'Phantom'. I can't wait to get tickets."

"You're going to love it."

"Oh, you've already seen it?"

"We saw it last week in preview."

"Didn't you just love it, darling. We saw it in London last year."

Sounds like, "Miss, Preview," just got out hoity-toitied.

****

A friend of mine sold his gas propane business and became a scillion-aire. Shortly thereafter,t he celebrated a major birthday. He threw a party. No, he threw an affair. It was grand. At the appropriate moment, all the children got up to praise, Dad. They laid on all the usual adjectives.....adoring, kind, loving, charitable, devoted, caring.....blah, blah, blah.

I thought the audience should hear from someone with no genetic or financial connection to, Dad. I got up. "Jack, I agree with everything your kids said. You deserve the success you've had. I don't begrudge you one penny of all the money you made in gas. But one thing does bother me. I've had gas all my life. The only difference between us is you sold yours. I just let mine go."

It was a gas!

****

We have a family friend who decided she needed a new outlet in life. She returned to the love of her youth. She would paint again. She found a studio and joined a class. She would start with a simple picture—a still life of a bowl of fruit.

She gathered a colorful array—bananas for yellow, a plum for purple, an apple for red, grapes for green. Her first session was pure pleasure. She looked forward to returning. But when she did, she was shocked. Someone had eaten her fruit.

Moral—beware those starving artists.

****

This is about the world's worst map. You won't find it in any Atlas or Rand McNally. It's on the airplane. It's that map that shows you the progress of your flight....where you're over. It uses a big plane flying over a small map. Take a flight New York to Miami. The back of the plane is over Delaware and the front is over North Carolina. So where am I over? If I'm sitting in the back, am I over Delaware? Are the people up front over North Carolina? They're going to get to Miami a lot sooner. I hope the pilot isn't using the same map.

****

I just have to close with one more "adorable." It's the Pop Pop in me. I was watching my little grandson playing tennis with a racket bigger than he. He was struggling. I yelled out to him, "Choke up! Choke up!" He stopped, dropped his racket and started to cough and choke.

It didn't help.

WHAT WAS... WUZ

You know what's hard getting used to? The "Used To's". You know the "Used To's." It's the way life used to be. It's the way we used to be.

We used to be thin.

We used to be taller because we used to be erect.

We used to have more hair, less stomach and no wrinkles.

We used to fall asleep without a pill.

We used to work.

We used to be stronger. Our drives used to reach the lake on the third hole.

We used to look at life differently. We used to think 65 was old and 75 was ancient.

Looking back, can you believe the lifestyle we used to live? We used to carouse 'til 2 a.m. and sleep 'til noon. We used to bake in the sun.....oiled up, no less! We used to have our steaks rare.....and often. We never used to need pills. We never heard of the word "cholesterol." And "HDL" was something you put in your car engine.

But best of all, remember when we used to.....<u>remember</u>?

But, perhaps, the most telling "Used To" is that doctor visit when the secretary used to hand you a clip board of papers to fill out. There was always that all encompassing question....."HAVE YOU EVER SUFFERED FROM".....followed by a list of 40 illnesses. Check "YES" or "NO."

You used to love that question. You wanted to show off. You used to fly down that " NO" column. This disease "NO". That disease "NO". Nothing but "NO", "NO", "NO." There was never a hesitation. Never a doubt. It was a shutout. A no-hitter! The NO's won 40-0. You were a rock! You were a specimen! And you didn't even have a personal trainer.

That's what used to be! Today the score might be 36-4 or 38-2. Today a lot of us have lost the shutout. So you lost your no-hitter. You'll get used to it. Hey, you're still in the game! You're still playing. You're way ahead. <u>You're here</u>!

That's easy to get used to.

BETWEEN THE SHEETS

There is an ebb and flow to life. We live our years in a very orderly progression. And we all seem to follow pretty much the same progression, marking the same milestones.

Take marriage. We mark off the years of our married lives with anniversaries and celebrations. We fill our photo albums with memories of births and birthdays. Every year there are more candles to blow out.....and more kids to blow out for. But truly the clearest, most vivid progression of our marriage can be found right in our bedroom. In fact, right in our beds.

Stage One. We are newlyweds. We are young and so in love. And how it shows. We are constantly kissing, touching and embracing. We are two feely, feelies. When we choose our first bed, there is no discussion, no difficult decision to mull over. Of course.....we shall sleep in a Queen size bed. We lie interlocked. Draped over each other. We can't sleep close enough. If they made Jack size beds, we'd have one.

Stage Two. We are not alone anymore. Little ones are now crawling into bed with us. Maybe a dog, too. One of us is always cold and gropes for more blanket. The other is always hot and keeps kicking the blanket away. In addition, the silence of sleep is now disturbed by the sound of a snore. The two feely, feely bodies are now getting a little touchy, touchy. They need their own space. The Queen must now abdicate her position to a King

<u>Stage Three:</u> We're older now and sleep doesn't come as easily as it once did. We're tossers and turners. One of us turns on a light and reads at 3 a.m.. Or maybe one of us watches late, late, late night TV. Or maybe one of us (you know who) spends more time in the bathroom than in bed.

We need even greater distance between us. You thought nothing could ever come between the two of you and now something has..... a night table! Twin beds.....the last bed stop.

Or is it?????

<u>Stage Four:</u> Fate deals you a surprise card. Suddenly you're single again. After awhile, you begin to date. You meet a great soul mate. A new bed mate. It's mutual. That feely, feely feeling is back and you're right back where you started.....in a cozy, cuddly Queen.

"Turn off the lights, honey."

TAKE A HIKE!

I guess there's nothing as wonderful as being a grandparent. Seeing those little ones grow and learn and develop is a wonder. And of course, if they're little Einstein's or A-Rod's, they've got your genes. But grand parenting has its tests.....one tough physical test, in particular. And I've been put to this test. I speak of that day when you must report for duty.....or lose your Pop Pop, Nana license. So tell your golf and tennis buddies you're not playing this Sunday. You're headed for camp visiting day!

It's about a 3 or 4 hour drive to our grandkids' camp. We try to leave about 6:30 a.m. so we can get in a full day. To save time, we pack some snacks.....no, we pack a breakfast.....no, we pack a mini banquet so we won't have to stop to eat. But it's the same story every year. We're only 30 minutes into the trip and the food is gone. We're eating before we even get out of the driveway. We've got 3 hours ahead with no food! To survive, we've been known to resort to cannibalism. We've raided the candy we're bringing the kids. (That's between us, please.)

All camps are built on the same plan Rome was built on.....seven hills. I don't think there is such a thing as a flat camp. The soccer field is always up the big hill.....basketball is half a mile up and then down that hill.....and the waterfront is at the bottom of a steep ski slope. Tell your cardiologist you walked from the waterfront, to your kid's bunk, to the baseball field and you won't have to take a stress test this year.

You took it!

Of course the first thing you look for when you arrive are your grandchildren. After big hugs and kisses, all you want to know is how they're doing. Are they happy? Do they like their bunk and counselor? All they want to know is what goodies you brought them.

After an hour of following them around, the only thing you're looking for is shade. It's always 90 something and very humid on visiting day. It's like being in, "Lawrence Of Arabia." All you want is a tree. You'll even take a very tall person to stand behind. In the height of this heat, you get a very special treat. You get to hike down to the waterfront.....sit out in the broiling sun and bake.....all while you watch your kids swim and frolic in cooling lake waters. You'd jump in, clothes and all, if you could.

If you're lucky, your kid has arts & crafts. For two straight periods! You're so proud of him. He's on his ninth laniard! If you're unlucky, your kid has a nature walk. You take a leisurely, educational stroll through flora and fauna while you furiously swat mosquitos. You'll scratch for a week.

The kids do get wonderful instruction.....golf, tennis, baseball, basketball. But on this day, you don't get to see your kid in any of these games. Today, you get to stand in an open field of half hay, under a burning sun and watch your kid in.....ARCHERY! He's a regular Robin Hood! One of his arrows almost reached the target! The archery counselor raves about your little one. "He's a natural. A born archer. He should pursue it." Where? How?

The counselors are great instructors but they never teach the kids lesson #1.....cleanliness, neatness. Every year my wife trudges up the hill to their bunk, hoping, praying, maybe this year, God willing, they got a counselor who can't live in a dirty, pig-sty-of-a-bunk. Maybe they got a counselor who will teach them about clean and neat. Every year it's the same.....the kids taught the counselor! Looking around the bunk, you can't tell which bed is the counselor's.

Parting is truly sweet sorrow. You'll miss them but you've had enough hiking. You can't wait to hit that AC button in your car. They'll miss you but they're happy to get back to their camp friends. So you hug and kiss goodbye and give them their candy.

What's left of it.

WILL POWER

I hardly know how to broach this subject. I'm afraid you might think it too depressing and leave. So let me slip into it gently. Someone once said there are only two sure things in life.....death and taxes. I think taxes is too depressing a subject. So let's talk about death.

Relax. Nobody is about to die. No, this is about an orderly preparation for that inevitable, far off day. And I'm not talking about buying more life insurance or coming to a free seminar (with food) to learn how you can double your estate and leave even more money to your kids and grandchildren and spoil them even more than you've already spoiled them and continue to spoil them. This is about the job of getting your estate in order.

This is where my wife shines. She is always ready for us to take on the job I hate most. "Honey, we have to meet with the lawyer and update our wills." For me, there are no more dreaded words than, update the will. The trickiest issues are usually not with your kids but how to take care of the grandchildren. And we have 7.

Take, Alex. My wife feels he is going astray down the wrong life path. "I'm afraid our inheritance could take all the drive out of, Alex. He could quit work and live like a bum and do nothing with his life." I have to remind her, "Honey, Alex could afford to go maybe 3 days without work on his allowance from our inheritance."

But our granddaughter, Alexy, is the one my wife is most concerned about. "Honey, I worry some fast talking Don Juan will come along and woo our Alexy off her feet. She's so impressionable. He'll marry her for her inheritance and then steal all her money. She will distrust men forever and never remarry. She'll grow old, alone and childless." I have to remind her, "Honey, we're here to write a will, not a TV mini-series."

At this point, the lawyer steps in to show off his expertise. "If that's a concern, perhaps you should leave the money in a trust and name a bank as the trustee. The bank will distribute the money as you direct in your will." My wife has a problem....."But suppose the kids have an emergency and need more money."

I explain....."They'll just have to plead their case with the banker."

"You want our kids to go beg a banker for their money?"

"Better than coming to us."

"They can't come to us. We're dead."

"Aren't we lucky."

And there are other concerns. When will the grandkids be old enough and mature enough to handle the money? It's particularly hard trying to judge that for our 11 month old, Johnathan. He can't even handle his bowels yet.

And then there's the great moral issue. If you financially helped one child more than the others, are you morally compelled to even the score and leave the others more? Who am I? Solomon? And of course there's always the killer.....which daughter-in-law gets which piece of jewelry? Even trickier if you have daughters-in-law and daughters. Thank, God, I won't be here for that divvy up.

When the lawyer gives us our final 30 page, "Last Will & Testament", which I know won't be our last, I always ask him for a one page summary in simple English. No legalese. Lawyers can't simply write, "You leave your money to your children." They can only say, "You bequeath your estate to your issue." It sounds like my wife gave birth to a *Time* magazine. Forget storks, the kid arrived in the mail box along with a *Newsweek*. As I think about it, "issue" is not a bad word because down the road, that's exactly what you're going to have with your issue.....issues! Big issues! Or as lawyers like to say....."From little issue, come big issues."

There's another reason why you can't get your lawyer to give you a simple summary. If you saw how simple it was to summarize those 30 pages, you'd never pay him the thousands he's billing you.

That could be an issue.

But then again, what the heck.....it's your issue's money!

2 BDRM. APT.

One of the most memorable sagas in life is the day we decide to sell our home. Just the thought of packing up 30 or 40 years of memories and junk, is enough to make some people stay put. And who wants all those strangers traipsing through your home.....looking, touching, snooping. And who knows when they'll show up. So your place must always be inspection ready.....beds made.....bathrooms clean.....kitchen spotless.....nothing lying around. (Most of all you!) Who can live so neat?

None of this deterred a friend of mine from selling his New York co-op apartment. Despite all his planning, he ran into a situation he never could have dreamed of or planned for.

Before he even got a broker, word got out that he was leaving the building. Apartment house word travels at the speed of gossip. Almost immediately, he got a call from his next door neighbor. "Next Door" wanted to buy his apartment. His plan was to breakthrough and make one grand layout.

My friend opened the deal with an asking price of $900,000. "Next Door" answered with a bid of $800,000. Thus began the "Negotiation Waltz":

> *"IF YOU COME UP A LITTLE*
> *I'LL COME DOWN A LITTLE*
> *AND LITTLE BY LITTLE*
> *WE'LL MEET IN THE MIDDLE"*

My friend told "Next Door" he was nowhere near a deal. He knew "Next Door" was drooling for his place. If he gets it, he doesn't have to move to a different building. No movers. No mess. And he doesn't have to sell his apartment. That was worth extra money.

On the other hand, "Next Door" figured he had the edge. He was saving the seller any agency commission. And on top of that, the seller wouldn't have hordes of nosy strangers trekking through his place. He played it smart. He upped his bid slightly to $825,000.

It was still not enough. To put a little more pressure on "Next Door," my friend held an Open House for brokers. About 30 showed up. The squeeze play worked. "Next Door" could smell a bidding war coming. To head it off, he went to $850,000. My friend dropped to $875,000. "Next Door" caved. It was a deal at $875,000.

The "Negotiation Waltz" was over. Or was it?

Now the sale had to be approved by the Co-Op Board. No problem. "Next Door" had already been approved by the Board. He already was a resident. Turns out <u>he</u> was okay.....but the deal wasn't. The Board nixed it because my friend wasn't getting enough money. The apartment was worth more. Like a good Board, they were keeping the value of their own places up.

My friend called "Next Door" and told him he had to negotiate with the Board. Whatever they decided was all right with him. He knew the price could only go north. And it did! The Board got him $25,000 more. And they didn't charge him a commission!

Go figure!

ABOUT FACE

Here is a scene I'm sure is being played out all over America. It is a meeting of man and woman, orchestrated by fate. It happens in a second—unforeseen and unexpected. The man could be just walking down the street. He turns the corner. Suddenly—wham!—bam!—she is standing before him. An old flame—no, an old torch—a white hot torch that still burns with passion. That face—how often it still floats through his dreams. That face—like a portrait by a master that hangs in his thoughts. Now after so many years, they stand face to face—awkward, uneasy, unsure. He looks—and looks—and looks. He is puzzled. That face is not the portrait in his mind. Finally he speaks—

THE MEETING

WHAT'S NEW?
I HARDLY RECOGNIZE YOU
WHAT BROUGHT ABOUT THE CHANGE
WHAT IN THE WORLD DID YOU DO TO YOU?

YOUR NOSE,
DARLING IT'S TOTALLY NEW
THAT'S NOT A LITTLE BOB
WHY DID YOU GO FOR THAT BIG A JOB?

YOUR EYES,
WHY ARE THEY OPENED SO WIDE?
DARLING I HATE TO THINK
WHAT KIND OF HELL YOU GO THROUGH TO BLINK
DON'T TRY TO WINK!

YOUR LIPS,
MY BUT THEY'RE FULL AND SO PLUMP
THEY LEAVE ME TOTALLY STUMPED
HOW DO YOU TAKE DAINTY SIPS
THROUGH THOSE LIPS?

YOUR FACE,
IT'S NOT THE FACE I ONCE KNEW
THERE'S NOT A LINE IN SIGHT
MAYBE THEY PULLED A LITTLE TOO TIGHT

MY DEAR,
WHERE IS YOUR TUMMY OF OLD?
THE ONE THAT I LOVED TO PAT
I DON'T RECALL IT—
AS FLAT AS THAT

MY, GOD,
EVERYTHING ON YOU IS NEW
THEREFORE I MUST SURMISE
YOU GOT YOURSELF A NEW SET OF THIGHS
IN YOUR FAVORITE SIZE

YOUR REAR,
WHERE'S THAT VOLUPTUOUS TUSH?
NOW WHEN YOU TAKE A SEAT
I HOPE YOU SIT YOUR TUSH ON A CUSH.

I'M SHOCKED,
MY HOW YOU'VE BLOSSOMED AND GROWN
YOU'RE LIKE A ROSE IN BLOOM
SINCE WHEN ARE YOU BUILT—
VA-VA-VA VOOM!

YOU'RE THROUGH,
THERE'S NOTHING MORE THEY CAN DO
I'VE LEARNED A LESSON FROM YOU
I'LL NEVER ASK A LADY—
WHAT'S NEW?

STRIP!

When you get up each morning, what's your routine? Do you hit the toothbrush first? Gotta wake up your mouth before you do another thing? Maybe you head straight for a hot shower. Your muscles and bones are crying, "Gimme heat!" Or maybe you're still in bed stretching your aching back. No matter what your routine, sooner or later you're going to have to face that moment of truth.

It could be good news or bad. It may be encouraging or depressing. I speak, of course, about that moment when you strip down to stark naked, cross your fingers, hold your breath and step on the scale.....oh so lightly.

With many older scales, the numbers spin around in a little window, like a Las Vegas slot machine, before they stop at your weight. I like this kind of scale because the numbers in the window are small and hard to read which allows me to get my weight more or less. And of course, like you, I always take the less. Some folks can't see the window over their stomach. Actually, that's a blessing. If you can't see the window over your stomach, you don't want to see the window.

Then there are those electronic talking scales where a stranger's voice inside the scale announces your exact weight. There's no margin for error here. No room for fudging. I don't think this is a popular scale. Who wants their weight announced out loud. The whole world doesn't have to know how much you've gained. I'll bet you ladies are embarrassed having a stranger in the bathroom with you while you're standing there naked.

Of course the most terrifying scale is the one in your doctor's office. No gimmicks…..just two super accurate weights for the nurse to balance. You have to get ready for this weigh in. Empty all your plumbing before you go. When the nurse tells you to step on the scale, you go into your routine. Start the "Stripper" music! Off with your shoes. Off with your shirt. Off with your belt. Empty your pockets. Out with the car keys, money, credit cards, chap stick, hankie. Off with your glasses. Off with your watch and bracelet. If it wasn't so complicated, you'd take out your contacts. And, of course, you always wear a pair of very light nylon shorts. Oops…..almost forgot. Off with your hair piece. Every milligram counts. You're like Sugar Ray before the big bout trying to get down to his weight limit.

I have a tip. Be nice to the nurse. Make friends. When she balances those weights, she never gets it exactly in the middle. There's room for negotiating here. You could negotiate her down half a pound. And if you're a regular Donald Trump, maybe even a pound. Think of what you have to go through to diet off a pound.

And of course, you know the best scale of all. The most accurate. The one that tells you exactly how you're doing weight wise. You don't step <u>on</u> it. You step <u>in</u> it.

Your pants!

WE CAN WORK IT OUT

I'm talking to you today from the gym—or if you live in a fancy neighborhood, the "Fitness Center"—so called because this is where people come to get a body their clothes will fit again. I see a man on the treadmill sweating profusely and visibly panting. I assume he's on there to help to lose his 40 pounds of overweight. I would say he's got another 10,000 miles to tread.

The women all come here to stay trim and fit and keep their girly figures. Looking around, I'd say it's working about 15% of the time. But it's not from lack of effort. These women are serious about their workouts. Just like professional athletes and Olympians, they put their bodies in the hands of a personal trainer. (That didn't come out right, did it?) Now what exactly do these personal trainers do for the women?

For one thing, they design a workout program for each lady's particular needs. Just as important, they gab, shmooz and gossip with the women during the workout. This is an invaluable service in helping the ladies get through the boredom of exercise. They also count reps for the ladies. That's repetitions, in gym talk.

You may well ask, how can trainers shmooz and count repetitions simultaneously? In trainer school, they not only have to learn the musculature of the human body and how all the muscles interact, which is task enough, they must also learn to compartmentalize their minds so they can talk and count simultaneously. That's why you never see a trainer chewing gum. That would be impossible.

But most important of all, a trainer makes the lady come to exercise regularly. Not by threat or force. Oh, no, they have a much more potent inducement. Once you book a trainer, you have to pay.....show or no show.....so you show!

The men are gyming it for a slightly different reason. They come to bulk up and build muscle strength. It's a man thing. The most dedicated are the guys who wear their T-tops with no sleeves. It's not that they can't afford sleeves, they just like to let their sinewy, muscled arms hang free for all to see, admire and envy. I call them the "Arms." A bit of advice. Don't shake hands with an "Arm" if you're a pianist or a puppeteer or if you teach sign language. Some of the "Arms" also wear their tops loose and scooped out low in the front. This allows for a peak of the pecs.

The "Arms" are also known as, "Barbellians." They work with barbells, the serious weightlifter's weights. The "Barbellians" emit an animalistic grunt as they lift. This is to make the barbell look heavier than it really is. Between the grunting and the sleeveless muscles, the "Barbellians" put on quite an audio/video show.

Most men wear normal T-shirts which reveal nothing.....because there is nothing worth revealing. (But there is much to hide.) They avoid the strain of barbells. They're no dumbells! They use the weight machines where never is heard a grunt or groan. I'm watching an interesting scenario take place. A man is waiting to use a weight machine. The lady on it is very muscular and obviously strong. She has the weight pin set all the way down to 6. That's a lot of weight. She now gets up and the man sits down. He looks around to make sure no one is watching and then casually pulls the pin out of 6 and moves it up to 3. There's no way he is going to let anyone see he was out-lifted by a lady. I guarantee, when he gets up he will casually drop the pin to 7 or 8 and walk away, hoping someone will notice his pumping prowess.

I guess weights build egos, too.

MAJOR HANG-UP

I have a question for all you ladies. Do you have enough closet space? If any of you feel perfectly satisfied with your closet space and wouldn't know what to do with one foot more, please step forward. Ah, I see the lady from the nudist colony stepped forward.

Suppose one day, the Closet Fairy appeared in your closet and offered to create for you any amount of closet space you desired with just a wave of her wand. Would you tell her, "Thank you, Closet Fairy, but I don't need any more space. It would just sit empty." Ha! Talk about fairy tales!

Ladies, admit it, when your kids left home for their own place, you moved into their closets before they even got out of the driveway. But then you missed the kids. So you filled that hole in your life with a cute, little, fluff-of-a-dog. This is why you see so many people walking dogs. A dog is the perfect replacement for departed children. A dog doesn't take up any closet space.

One reason your closet is inadequate is all the different size wardrobes you keep. And each size has its own section. And each section has its own name. At one end is your, **"This Is Why He Married Me"** rack. At the opposite end, is your, **"This Is Why I'm Not Going Back To My High School Reunion"** rack. In between is your, **"How My Tailor Retired So Young"** section.

And, of course, the real problem with you ladies and gentlemen is your inability to throw anything out. Your closets are filled with brand new, never-opened-still-got-the-tags-on them outfits you've never worn. "How can I throw out something I've never worn?" You've got to.....to make room for all that new stuff you're going to buy and never wear.....or even open!

Now let's be honest. How much of your clothing do you really wear? You North/South, back-and-forthers have it the worst. Every winter you ship wardrobes of clothing down here. You never wear half the stuff. Come the summer, you put the same clothing you didn't wear down here, back into the same wardrobes, and ship it back up north where you'll still never wear it. You just keep shipping the same stuff back and forth. Incredible! Your clothes lead the same great life you do. You should come back one of your jackets!

What really sums up this dilemma best, is madam's cry when she's in her closet getting ready for a big night out. She let's out a sigh and then in a "What-am-I-going-to-do" cry, she appeals to anyone who will listen.....

"I HAVE NOTHING TO WEAR!!!!!!!"
Hah!

FUNNY YOU SHOULD ASK

Of all the questions we ask each other, which one do you think is asked most often? I think the most popular question—without question—is, "How are you?" How many times a day do you greet a friend, a neighbor, an acquaintance, a fellow worker—"Hello, how are you?" It's hard to say, "Hello," without immediately asking, "How are you?" They're attached. They're Siamese greetings.

"How are you" shows caring on our part, although we really aren't asking for a medical report. It's so automatic, we often ask, "How are you," without really wanting to know how the person is. Many times, we don't even listen to their answer.

"How are you, Peter?"

"I'm going in for surgery tomorrow."

"That's nice."

Yes, "How are you?" is a custom—a habit—a formality—a nicety we want to get rid of quickly. It rolls off our tongue like shorthand—"How R U?"

"Hey, good to see you, Jack, how R U?"

Then your question boomerangs back to you.

"I'm good, Gordon, how R U?"

We're such a caring people always asking each other, "How R U?" What's interesting are our answers.

"How R U, Betty?"

"I'm OK."

OK is just OK. It's non committal. It's like getting "satisfactory" on your term paper.

"How R U, Alan?"

"I'm good." "Good" is good. It's not great but it's good enough. It means there are no pressing problems or medical issues to be discussed. We can get on with the conversation. Whew!

"How R U, Frank?

"Not bad."

Well, we really don't know how Frank is, do we? Is he hiding something? He's certainly not as good as, Alan, who was "Good," He's not even as good as, Betty, who was just "Okay". But all things considered, his "Not bad" is really—not bad. Frank is a B or B minus. He could even be a C, depending on his complexion. But looked at another way, "Not bad" sounds very good compared to, "Not good." Everyone, including Frank, would rather be "Not bad" than "Not good." It's one of those quirky times in our language when "Bad" is better than "Good."

Beware whom you ask, "How R U?" I'm sure you have friends, like I have, who think you really want to know. They've got answers that will make you sorry you ever asked, "How R U?".

"I don't think I'm still contagious."

"I'm going for a fourth opinion tomorrow."

"I'll know when my tests come back"

And then there are the two words you cringe to hear:

"How R U, Phyllis?"

"Don't ask!"

"Don't ask" means, "Ask!" It also means, "I would have told you even if you hadn't asked." You're trapped. Get ready for an earful. You must learn there are certain people you never ask, "How R U?" To avoid the "Don't ask" trap—don't ask!

Not only do we greet each other on a caring note, we part on one, too. "Good to see you, Don. Have a good day." That's a nice wish. I use it all the time.....but I spice it up. If we should ever meet, I'll bid you farewell my way:

"Have a good day—and an even <u>better</u> night!"

IT'S A CRIME

Maybe it's just me, but nighttime TV has gone cop crazy. Every channel I flick to, it's the same scene. Detectives, surrounded by that ubiquitous yellow crime tape, peering down at the remains of another victim. And then there are those new age crime fighters—Sherlockian wonders—the Crime Scene Investigators. Armed with only tweezers, they gather the minutest, microscopic clues—clues that will identify and convict the true killer by the DNA of his nasal hairs. Maybe "crime doesn't pay" but it sure pays for the networks. These nights, prime time—is crime time.

I have watched so many TV trials, I could now prosecute or defend any defendant. I know my way around the law—change of venue, the art of the cross exam, plea bargaining, first, second, third degree—I know the tricks! And I don't have a law degree. I learned my law better. I learned it nights on Network U.

I have also lived <u>real</u> life crime. My first run in with the bad guys came one night while we were out of town. Our house was well alarmed. Every window and door was wired. I was ready for them. Well, I should have known better. What crook comes in through the doors or windows? They crawled into our bedroom through a hole in the wall. How did the hole get there? They put it there.

They were not interested in TV's or stereos. They were after a safe. They found it in my wife's closet. But I was smart. I had it bolted to the wall. Just try to get that out. They didn't even try. They just knocked a hole in the wall and pulled out the safe still attached to a hunk of wall. They came well tooled for the job. I called them the "Carpenter Crooks."

Now, how were they going to get this heavy safe (and wall) to their car a few miles away? By car, of course. Whose car? My car! They found my car keys in the kitchen and took off for the nearest safe cracker. But they were neat. They closed the garage doors.

It took a while for us to recover from the chilling effect of knowing strangers had been in our house—in our bedroom! Had they tried our bed? Had they used our bathroom? My wife threw away the bedding and had the bathroom blasted clean. We never got the carpeting fully clean from fingerprint dust. But eventually, our lives returned to normal.

Bring on Act II.

Again we were out of town and would you believe it—the "Carpenter Crooks" came back for more. Did they like our bed? Did they love our toilet? They started banging a new hole in our bedroom wall in the same spot. This time I was the smart one. When I had their first hole rebuilt, I had it reinforced with metal sheathing. As they banged away in frustration, my neighbor heard the hammering. She alerted the police. They came and the crooks fled. But this is the part I love.

The police sent one patrolman. He parked a few houses down the block. It was a very dark night and as he walked up to my house gun drawn, he actually bunked into their lookout man. They collided! The lookout yelled to the "carpenters" and they all beat it into the woods. I asked the policeman why he didn't shoot the lookout on the spot. He said he couldn't unless he caught him in the house, in the act. We really protect our crooks. But then again, it's a good thing they didn't get him in the house. There would have been blood all over the carpet.

The story has a good "crime-doesn't-pay" ending. They finally caught these "Carpenter Crooks" and sent them to prison.

Watch your walls, Warden.

MAD. AVE MADNESS

So you think advertising is nothing more than a bunch of guys sitting around brainstorming. Let me take you on a trip behind the advertising scene and show you a world you've never seen. Not even on, "Mad Men."

The following story is true. No names have been changed to protect the innocent because I don't mention any names. This is a tale about winning new business.....the lifeline of any agency. We were one of 3 agencies pitching a large, prestigious national account.....well into 8 figures. A day or two before the presentation, a friend who had worked on the business at another agency, called me with a note of caution. Their head man, their marketing director, was a real serious, stone face. All business. No laughs. Get right down to work. I immediately switched my wardrobe to a dark blue suit and red tie. I told all my people to show up very Brooks Brothers.

Whenever I had an important 9 a.m. meeting like this, I would stay in New York overnight so I wouldn't have to worry about traffic. My wife often joined me. Kept me calm. On this night, we were staying right across the street from my office. What could possibly go wrong? Funny you should ask.

I got up at 7, proceeded to the bathroom and turned on the water. No water in the sink. Bone dry. I tried the shower. Not a drop. My blood pressure rose. I couldn't even brush my teeth. I called the front desk.

"I'm sorry, Mr. Bushell, but there's been a water main break. There's no water in the hotel."

They couldn't tell me how long before water flowed again. I called another hotel down the block. They had water but they were using a water tank on their roof. They didn't know how long it would last. I couldn't chance it. I called a hotel about 12 blocks uptown. They had water and a room. I booked it!

I grabbed my stuff—told my wife to meet me there and flew out the door. When I checked in, I told the lady that a pretty blond (she still is) would be by in about 20 minutes asking for me. Just send her to my room. I got one of those "dirty old man" looks. I told her it was my wife. I got one of those, "I've heard that before" looks. I gave her one of those, "I only wish" looks.

I raced up to my room, showered, shaved, dressed, and raced downstairs for a cab. Too long a line. Couldn't wait. Had to walk. No, run! I ended up half trotting so I wouldn't sweat. All I could think of was, "Well into 8 figures, Gordon, keep pushing."

Got to my lobby about 8:55. Five minutes to spare. As the elevator doors closed, I noticed 4 men entering the lobby all suited, tied and attached, led by "Stone Face"—and he looked it. It was them! I was one elevator ahead. I got to my floor and raced to the conference room. My people wanted to know what had happened to me. No time to explain. I had to bring in the clients.

I tried to settle down and get my bearings while we all had some coffee and danish. When everyone was seated and ready to begin, I asked them how their morning had gone so far. They were all doing fine. "Stone Face" just nodded. You could see he just wanted to get on with business and skip any small talk.

I decided to take a chance. "Well, gentleman, let me tell you how my morning has gone." I described it blow by blow. The bone dry sink and shower—the frantic calls—the race uptown—the race back downtown—the 1 elevator lead. As my plight unfolded, I could see the stone on "Stoneface" was starting to crack and by the time I got to my "dirty old man" check-in, it was shattered and he was laughing. Being a true salesman, I used my story as a sales pitch. I told them, more than anything else they would hear this morning, my plight proves our agency gets the job done no matter what the obstacle.

We got the business. I've often thought, suppose "Stoneface" had not enjoyed my crazed quest for hot water?

I could have been in hot water.

IT COULD HAVE BEEN "GIVINGTHANKS"

As I sit here writing this, the calendar is slowly ticking its way to November. Ah, November—the last in that poetic refrain, "Thirty days hath September." With November, also comes election time—the clamor and clatter of politicians fill the air. There's something else in the November air—the first feel of wintry winds.

But nothing says November like that special day—no, that glorious holiday—Thansgiving! So let's not waste any time. Let's get right to it. Let's talk turkey. It's Thanksgiving! Time for stuffing, cranberries and yummy yams. It's such a wonderful time of the year. I'll tell you one thing we can all be thankful for. We're not turkeys! They have nothing to give thanks for.

I wonder what that first Thanksgiving dinner was like. Did the Pilgrims have any idea they were starting a national holiday—an American institution? Did the Indians think this was just another "make nice" invitation.

What kind of an affair was it? Did they send the Indians invitations? Or did they just walk over and ask them to drop by for dinner?

And what time was it called for? They could have picked any time. There was no football game. There were no Detroit Lions. In fact, there was no Detroit! So once the Indians all got there, what did the hostess serve for hors d'oeuvres? Did she even serve hors d'oeuvres? They didn't have franks in a blanket back then. And after dinner, do you think the

Indians offered to help with the dishes? Do you think they brought a little gift for the hostess? I'll bet they did. They made beautiful beaded jewelry.

And how did the Pilgrims decide on serving turkey? They didn't know it at the time, but that was a momentous decision. For example, they could have served ham or beef or fish. The symbol for this holiday could have been a pig, a cow or a scrod. The turkeys would have loved that. They would have gladly given up being "poster boy" for this great holiday. I think the one factor that swung it over to turkey may have been cholesterol.

I wonder what the reaction was when the hostess brought out the turkey. Did the Indians groan to themselves, "Oh, no—not turkey again." Were they hoping for a steak or maybe a veal chop? I can commiserate with them. This may be unpatriotic to say just before Thanksgiving, but I'm tired of turkey.

I eat turkey almost every day of the year. I have it on sandwiches, in salads, in wraps, in burgers. I have if for lunch—for dinner—for snacking. I'm beginning to develop a double neck. I'm thinking of writing a letter to the *Guiness World Book Of Records*. I think I have a shot at the most consecutive days eating turkey. When I really get tired of turkey, for a change of pace, I switch to chicken. Some change of pace. Chicken is a small turkey.

There's an interesting similarity between us and turkeys. On Thanksgiving Day, they go gobble, gobble, gobble and end up stuffed. We sit down at the table and go gobble, gobble, gobble and end up stuffed. Among my many Thanksgiving blessings, I give thanks for my perfect turkey mate. My wife loves the dark meat and I love the white.

We make beautiful gobble.

And now the finale, Maestro...

BACH N' ROLL

Johann Sebastian Bach stands as one of the giants in classical music. Did you know his favorite form was the cantata? You probably couldn't even **spot-a-cantata** if you heard one. Don't be embarrassed. The music world has totally **forgot-a-cantata**. But oh, how Bach loved to compose cantatas. He'd be sitting home on a Sunday morning and the phone would ring. It was the King calling. "Hey, Jo"—that was short for Johann. "I'm throwing a party at the castle in 2 weeks. You **got-a-cantata**?" Bach would sit at the piano and begin to **jot-a-cantata**. In no time he'd get back to the king. "Relax, King, have I **got-a-cantata** for you.

He wrote cantatas everywhere. One summer he and his wife took a cruise to Spain. He loved the food. Came home and wrote, **"Cantata Enchalada."** The next summer they toured Italy. The food was even better. You guessed it.....**"Cantata Picata."** His wife loved the Italian fashions. She came back from shopping one day all excited. "Oh, Jo, (short for Johann)—have I **got-a-cantata** for you! You must write this.....a **"Cantata-to-Prada."**

But Bach was not into fashion. What he loved most of all in Italy was the language. It was so lyrical—a symphony of vowels. People spoke and he heard music. One day in Florence, on the Ponte Veccio, while his wife went crazy shopping, he just stood there drinking in the language all around him. He heard notes and passages in his head. They took form and shape as he began to **plot-a-cantata**. From that magic moment on the Ponte Veccio, came one of his biggest hits—"Hey, **What's-A-Da-Matta-Cantata.**" I would say, in its time, there was no **hotta-cantata**.

Bach was the foremost cantata teacher in Europe. There was a 5 year wait to get into his class. And he was a tough teacher. He told his students exactly what he thought of their work. Like the day young Hans came to Bach's studio to play his cantata composition for the master. He was nervous. But with every note he played, his courage and enthusiasm grew. When the cantata was over, Bach walked slowly to the piano, put his hand on Hans' shoulder and said, "Hans, you call **dat-a-cantata?**"

If you're interested in hearing some cantata music, I recommend an event held every summer in Liepzig—the **"Liepzig Cantata Regatta."** As they say in their brochure—**"Come To Liepzig For A Lotta Cantata."**

Many consider Liepzig the home of the Bach cantata. The Liepzig opera house is where many new Bach cantatas premiered. These premieres were always the social highlight of the year. Magnificent golden, gilded carriages, pulled by teams of pure white steeds, arrived with Liepzig's hoity toityest. Men stepped out wrapped in swirling black capes—draped over svelte, silk cutaways and all topped off with formal black opera hats. They were followed by magnificent women with every strand of hair coiffed to perfection. And oh! the gowns. Every top European designer was represented. One was more breathtaking than the other. Indeed, there was an unwritten rule in Liepzig society and it was sacrosanct.....**"Never Wear A Shmata-To-A-Cantata."**

The Liepzig Opera House is also where a most unusual cantata tradition began. At the end of the cantata performance, the audience would not applaud. Rather, they paid Bach special homage. They rose to their feet and in perfect unison, as though led by an invisible conductor, the audience would utter in awed reverence—three times—**"What-A-Cantata"**—**"What-A-Cantata"**—**"What-A-Cantata."**

And now, friends, I feel like Bach must have felt as he put down the final note of a new cantata. Emotionally spent and exhausted. I must close now.

I'm out-a-cantata.

I hope you enjoyed our time together. I had a good laugh—laughing at myself. I hope you had a good laugh on yourself. Keep that laugh in your heart and that smile on your face. Most of all, when things aren't going great, look for the humor. It's there somewhere—tucked away—ready to rear its funny head. That's what makes humor a funny thing.

Did I already say that?